A Holy Life

The Writings of Saint Bernadette of Lourdes

PATRICIA McEACHERN, Ph.D.

A HOLY LIFE

The Writings of
Saint Bernadette of Lourdes

IGNATIUS PRESS   SAN FRANCISCO

Interior art:
All photographs and descriptive text in captions were provided by
the archives of St. Bernadette Institute of Sacred Art,
Albuquerque, New Mexico

Cover art: Detail of a photograph by Father Bernadou
taken in 1862 when Bernadette was eighteen

Cover design by Riz Boncan Marsella

ISBN 978-1-58617-116-2
Library of Congress Control Number 2005927347
Printed in the United States of America ∞

For the Very Reverend
Monsignor John Henry Westhues
Priest, Spiritual Director and Friend

My soul proclaims the greatness of the Lord;

My spirit rejoices in God my Savior.

For he has looked with favor on his lowly servant.

—Magnificat (Luke 1:47–48a)

CONTENTS

ACKNOWLEDGMENTS

One of my greatest pleasures is expressing gratitude, and I enjoy a unique opportunity here to thank the many friends and colleagues who have generously assisted me in this project. Most importantly, I would like to express my great appreciation to the Very Reverend Monsignor John Henry Westhues for serving as my spiritual director and for being a steadfast example of holiness.

Père Bertrand Ponsard, C.M., of the Chapel of the Miraculous Medal, rue du Bac, Paris, has my eternal gratitude. Without his help at a crucial moment, this book would not have been written. I am extremely grateful to the Carmelite Sisters of Springfield, Missouri for their help with religious terminology, for their kindness and for their prayers. I also appreciate the hospitality and the assistance of the Sisters of Charity and Christian Instruction at Saint-Gildard Convent in Nevers, France.

A woman whom I met at a conference at Franciscan University brought Saint Bernadette's writings to my attention. Unfortunately, I do not know her name, but should she ever read these pages, I would like her to know that I am grateful to her. Larry Sloan, owner of DeSales Catholic Bookstore, and Samantha Lovetere, his gracious assistant, helped me to track down information that I needed. I also appreciate their encouragement and their interest in this project.

I am indebted to Dr. Elaine Roer Westhues and Monsignor John Henry Westhues for their help in translating Latin passages into English. Sister Barbara Dingman, of the Daughters of Charity of Saint Vincent de Paul, rue du Bac, helped me with religious terminology. I appreciate the encouragement I received from Father Mike McDevitt, Pastor of Saint Agnes Cathedral, in Springfield, Missouri. Ruben Care and Autumn, Jess, Jonah and Agnes Sweley supported this project with their prayers, their interest and their encouragement.

I would like to express my appreciation to Drury University for granting me a sabbatical to work on this project. Special thanks go to my colleagues Dr. Resa Willis, Dr. Steven Good, Dr. Charles Taylor, Dr. Rebecca Barck, Dr. Patrick Moser, Dr. John E. Moore, Kathy Daniels and the Board of Trustees for their encouragement, support and practical assistance.

I am indebted to everyone at Ignatius Press who has worked with me to bring Saint Bernadette's book to print. All have my heartfelt gratitude. Special thanks go to Father Joseph Fessio, S.J., Editor. Penelope Boldrick has my sincere appreciation for her prayers and her cheerful assistance. I appreciate the meticulous attention of the copy editor, Emily Zomberg Ayala and the proofreader as well. I thank Eva Muntean for her patience.

In addition, I am grateful for the help, support and encouragement of Most Reverend John J. Leibrecht, Bishop of Springfield-Cape Girardeau Diocese, Father Marek Bozek, Johnny Faulkner, Rosie Homan, Michael Thomas, Dr. Martine Rey, Lynn McEachern, Majel Boree McEachern, Tim McEachern, Jean Peeden, Agatha Farmer, Darice Augustan, Mary Holke, Amanda Neal, Father David Hulshof, Nennele de Flores, Ann Rice, Dr. Stirling Haig, Dr. Jose Polo de Bernabe, Tynes Emory Mixon, M.D., Dr. Karl-Heinrich Barsch, and Bruno Gargiolo.

Finally and most importantly, I wish to acknowledge and thank Our Lady of Lourdes and Saint Bernadette for their intercession.

INTRODUCTION

On a cold winter day in 1858 in Lourdes, France, Bernadette Soubirous, a tiny, asthmatic shepherdess went in search of wood along the Gave River. The vision this humble young girl experienced that day has since deepened the faith of millions. Bernadette could scarcely believe her eyes when a beautiful Lady appeared before her. Eventually, she would come to understand that it was the Holy Virgin Mary herself who had appeared to her that day and on seventeen subsequent occasions. Church authorities could not have been expected to believe immediately that the Virgin Mary had appeared in a grotto where pigs took shelter from the thunderstorms that sometimes raged through the countryside surrounding the small village in the Pyrenees. Even more unlikely was that she would have enlisted the aid of a poverty-stricken, uneducated girl whose family had been reduced to living in a former jail cell condemned as too unhealthy even to house prisoners. It was highly improbable that the Immaculate Conception herself would choose this fourteen-year-old girl whose own living conditions were so very far from immaculate. Bernadette understood that the Blessed Mother had demonstrated great humility in appearing to her, conversing with her and asking for her aid, and asking so kindly and respectfully. Bernadette would spend the rest of her brief life trying to follow the example of humility that the Queen of Heaven herself had shown to her.

The story of Saint Bernadette Soubirous of Lourdes has exerted a powerful influence on the spiritual lives of millions of people for a century and a half. Scores of writers, be it scholarly, religious or secular, have written about Saint Bernadette and her visions of the Holy Virgin Mary at the Grotto of Massabielle. Bernadette is typically portrayed as an honest, but illiterate and uncatechised young girl, as she was at the time of the apparitions. The catechist who prepared her for her First Communion went so far as to claim that she was incapable of learning, and Father Pomian, her confessor, accurately referred to her as a *tabula rasa*, that is, a blank slate. Indeed, she was thoroughly uneducated when the Holy Virgin Mary first appeared to her. Hence, it comes as a surprise even to her most ardent *dévotés* that in reality Bernadette became a prolific letter writer; she even corresponded with Pope Pius IX to ask for his apostolic blessing. In addition to her letters, Bernadette compiled a tiny anthology of *Private Notes* in which she carefully recorded quotes, reflections, prayers and spiritual advice. More than any other document, her *Private Notes* offers a glimpse into the profound spiritual life of this "most secret of saints". Her letters were not collected and published in the original French until the late twentieth century and they are translated into English here for the first time.

Saint Bernadette is as relevant now as she was in 1858 because the message of Lourdes is *conversion*, and Bernadette lived that message. On August 14 and 15, 2004, Pope John Paul II made his second papal visit and pilgrimage to Lourdes to celebrate the 150th anniversary of the proclamation of the Immaculate Conception as dogma. The year 2008 marks the one hundred and fiftieth anniversary of the apparitions when the Holy Virgin appeared to Bernadette and confirmed this dogma with the words: "I am the Immaculate Conception." An uncatechised *tabula rasa* like fourteen-year-old Bernadette Soubirous would not have heard the expression "Immaculate Conception" in the tiny, isolated mountain village of Lourdes. When Bernadette told Father Peyramale, her parish priest, that the Lady who appeared to her in the Grotto had identified herself with these words, he responded that she could not have said such a thing because conception is an event, and a person cannot be an event. Nevertheless, this expression is a grammatical parallel of the words of Jesus Christ himself when he said: "I am the resurrection and the life." These expressions are grammatically illogical, yet spiritually true. How could an uneducated shepherdess have made such a grammatical parallel on her own, a fascinating parallel that evidently her parish priest did not recognize?

Saint Bernadette continues to attract millions of pilgrims to the French towns of Lourdes and Nevers, just as she did when she was living. Each year, thousands of pilgrims pray before her incorrupt body at the chapel of Saint-Gildard, the convent in Nevers where she lived and died. Since the time of Bernadette's visions, Lourdes has become the most frequented Marian shrine in Europe and is one of the greatest healing centers of the world. It boasts an average of one authenticated miraculous cure every two years (the latest in 1999) as well as thousands of cures that either cannot be investigated by the Medical Bureau or cannot pass its uncompromising standards. In 1990, so many pilgrims visited Lourdes that a "holy-water shortage" was temporarily declared, and for the first time in its history there was rationing. An unlikely ensemble of authors and periodicals have written about Saint Bernadette Soubirous and the healing waters of Lourdes, including the *New York Times*, William F. Buckley, Jr., *Time Magazine*, *The Economist*, Emile Zola, J.-K. Huysmans, François Mauriac and Franz Werfel. A wistful and reverent example of Bernadette's continuing influence is evident in Leonard Cohen's plaintive folksong entitled "The Song of Bernadette", in which he pays tribute to the visionary in an intensely personal way. The story of Bernadette Soubirous and the "beautiful Lady" of her visions has captivated people for one hundred and fifty years, but until now we have only been able to know her through articles, books, films and songs. At last we have the opportunity to meet Bernadette through her own words.

When the cause for canonization was opened for Saint Bernadette, it was due in large part to her popularity as an exemplary model for Christians seeking to live a devout life. It is only in her writings, however, that we can begin to see past her veil of secrecy and realize the depth of her spirituality. It is true that Bernadette is famous for her extraordinary experience of having been favored with visions of the Holy Virgin and because of her participation in bringing forth the spring that would heal many; however, the story of her courageous struggle for holiness is perhaps even more extraordinary than her visions. At the age of eleven, she contracted cholera, a disease that stunted her growth permanently. She never grew any taller than the child-like height of approximately 4 feet 7 inches. In addition, the ravages of cholera left her with severe, chronic asthma and eventually she contracted tuberculosis of the lungs and bones. She was given last rites on four different occasions. Bernadette suffered terribly for many years before her death at the age of thirty-five, but her response to suffering was genuinely heroic. This humble, self-effacing nun transformed excruciating suffering into spiritual fecundity. Her letters and *Private Notes* serve as a model for those who are passing through their own trials. Bernadette's writings are permeated with her strong desire for humility, her ever-present expressions of gratitude and her deep appreciation and love for the Eucharist. They reveal an intimate and profound love for God the Father, Jesus and Mary. Anyone interested in pursuing a deeper spiritual life or in knowing Bernadette as she truly was and in her own words will appreciate the person that the pages of this volume reveal: a humble soul, with her own human frailties, who sought holiness.

CHAPTER I

Journal Dedicated to the Queen of Heaven

On May 12, 1866, Bernadette lovingly penned the title "Journal Dedicated to the Queen of Heaven" in a large yellow notebook. It was decorated with a picture of Jesus beside a group of children and a banner that read: "Let the children come unto me." With tender expressions of love, humility and gratitude, Bernadette spoke directly to the Most Holy Virgin, but she asked the Queen of Heaven essentially for one thing alone: help in serving her and her Son. What follows Bernadette's two introductory paragraphs in the "Journal" is the beginning of her account of the events at Massabielle.

Unfortunately, she never completed this section. Seven weeks after beginning her "Journal", she left for the Convent of Saint-Gildard in Nevers, leaving the notebook behind in Lourdes.

Bernadette wrote and signed numerous accounts of her visions. In addition, she underwent repeated interrogations by both ecclesial and civil authorities, during which her testimony was transcribed. In none of these accounts did she contradict herself; on the other hand, there is no one single version that includes every detail. In order to give the most complete picture possible of the events surrounding her visions in her own words, the following version is a compilation; however, every individual sentence was either spoken or penned by Bernadette herself.

This account of the apparitions and the subsequent police interrogations comes from letters and journals written five to eight years after the visions, between 1861 and 1866. Bernadette's focus always remained on the substance of the visions: humility, penance and conversion. In her written accounts, Bernadette twice stated that the request to have a chapel built occurred during the third apparition, when in fact Our Lady made this request for the first time during the ninth. In addition, after going into great detail about the first and second apparitions, when she reached the third, she habitually summed up the details of the following apparitions rather than recounting exactly what happened when. Although she was impeccably accurate in recounting the apparitions when they occurred, with the passing of the years, the dates and the order of the apparitions were less important to her. What was important for Bernadette was to live the message of Massabielle.[1]

Journal Dedicated to the Queen of Heaven

May 12, 1866

Dearest Mother, how happy was my soul those heavenly moments when I gazed upon you. How I love to remember those sweet moments spent in your presence, your eyes filled with kindness and mercy for us! Yes, dear Mother, your heart is so full of love for us that you came down to earth to appear to a poor, weak child and convey certain things to her despite her great unworthiness. How humbled she is. You, the Queen of Heaven and Earth, chose to use what is weakest in the eyes of men. O Mary, give the precious virtue of humility to she who dares to call herself

[1] For a more detailed account of the apparitions, the reader should refer to the Chronology.

your child. O loving Mother, help your child resemble you in everything and in every way. In a word, grant that I may be a child according to your heart and the heart of your dear Son.

You know that my dearest desire is to consecrate myself in religious life so that I may better serve you and your dear Son. I am placing all my intentions under your holy protection and I beg you to remove whatever obstacles may exist, for you can do this better than anyone.

Apparitions of the Holy Virgin at the Grotto

The first time I went to the Grotto was Thursday, February 11, 1858. I was going to collect wood with two other girls[2] and we went in the direction of the Grotto.[3] When we reached the mill, I asked them if they wanted to go see where the water from the mill joined the Gave.[4] They said yes. We followed the canal and when we got there, we found ourselves before a Grotto. Since we could go no farther, my two companions began to cross the stream in front of the Grotto, and I was there alone on the other side.[5] They started crying, and I asked them why. They answered that it was because the water was cold.[6] I asked the other girls

[2] The other two girls were Bernadette's sister, Marie, and a friend by the name of Jeanne Abadie.

[3] The source of the account thus far is Bernadette's *Journal Dedicated to the Queen of Heaven.*

[4] Bernadette is referring to the Gave River.

[5] These lines are taken from an account of the apparitions written for Father Charles Bouin on August 22, 1864.

[6] This comes from the account of the apparitions written for Father P. Ferdinand Gondrand of the Oblates of Mary-Immaculate in Bétharram. It is dated May 28, 1861.

to throw some stones in the water to help me see if I could cross without removing my shoes.[7] They said that if I wanted to cross the stream, I could do as they had done.[8] I went a little farther to see if there was a place where I could cross without removing my shoes, but it was no use.

Scarcely had I removed my first stocking,[9] when I heard a noise like a sudden gust of wind.[10] When I turned my head toward the prairie, I saw that the trees were not swaying at all, so I began removing my stockings again. I heard the same noise again. When I raised my head and looked at the Grotto, I saw a Lady[11] in white.[12] She was wearing a white gown with a blue sash, a white veil and a golden rose on each foot,[13] the same color as the chain of her Rosary, which had white beads.[14] She was surrounded with white light, but it was not a blinding light.[15] She had blue

[7] *Journal.* The water would have been extremely cold in February. Since Bernadette suffered from a very serious case of asthma, she learned to be careful about catching cold.

[8] Father Bouin. Quoted in André Ravier, ed. *Les Écrits de Sainte Bernadette et sa voie spirituelle* (hereafter cited as ESB).

[9] What Bernadette refers to as her "stockings" were in fact long, thick woolen socks. Because of the family's poverty, these stockings would normally have been considered a luxury rather than a necessity. Bernadette only enjoyed this "luxury" because of her delicate health.

[10] *Journal* (quoted in ESB).

[11] When Bernadette was finally literate, thus able to write the account of the apparitions, she wrote either "a Lady" or "the Holy Virgin". When she first talked about the visions, however, she described the Holy Virgin as the "tiny maiden" or "that" ["that one"].

[12] Father Bouin (quoted in ESB).

[13] The Lady was barefoot, except for the golden roses.

[14] Father Gondrand (quoted in ESB).

[15] This is taken from a letter written to an unidentified man (Monsieur) in 1866. In this letter, Bernadette clarified some details of the apparitions and corrected some misinformation that was printed in a brochure entitled *Une visite à la Grotte et à Bernadette.*

eyes.[16] When I first saw her, I was a little bit afraid. Thinking that what I was seeing was an illusion, I rubbed my eyes, but it made no difference: I still saw the same Lady. So I put my hand in my pocket and took out my Rosary. I tried in vain to make the sign of the cross;[17] I was not able to raise my hand to my forehead. When I realized this, I froze completely in fear. The Lady took the Rosary she was holding between her hands and she made the sign of the cross.[18] Then I tried a second time and this time I was able do it.[19] Immediately after I had made the sign of the cross, the great fear that had seized me disappeared. I knelt and prayed the Rosary, in the presence of this beautiful Lady.[20] She passed the beads of her Rosary[21] between her fingers, but she did not move her lips.[22] When I finished praying the Rosary, she made a sign to me to draw near to her, but I did not dare.[23] Then she suddenly disappeared.[24]

I removed my other stocking to cross the stream in front of the Grotto, and we left. Along the way, I asked my friends if they had seen anything. They answered, "No. And how about you? Did you see something?" I said, "Oh no. If you didn't see anything, I didn't see anything either." I did not want to tell them what I had seen, but they were so insistent that I decided to if they promised not to breathe a

[16] Father Bouin (quoted in ESB).

[17] *Journal* (quoted in ESB).

[18] This comes from a letter written to an unidentified woman (Madame) around 1865.

[19] *Journal* (quoted in ESB).

[20] Father Bouin (quoted in ESB).

[21] Father Gondrand (quoted in ESB).

[22] *Journal* (quoted in ESB).

[23] Father Bouin (quoted in ESB).

[24] *Journal* (quoted in ESB).

word of it to anyone.[25] They thought that she wanted to do us harm, so they said I should not go back there again and neither should they. I told them no.[26] They promised to keep the secret, but no sooner did they get home than they rushed to tell what I had seen.[27] So that was the first time.[28]

Even though my mother had forbidden me to go back to the Grotto, I returned for the second time on the following Sunday because something inside me drew me there. After Mass, I asked my mother if I could go back. She did not want me to go because she was afraid I would fall in the water or I would be late for Vespers. I promised her that I would be back in time, and she finally gave me permission to go.[29] I went with several other girls, thinking that perhaps I had been mistaken about what I saw.[30] I went to the church to fill a small bottle with holy water to throw on the vision if I saw her again. I did indeed see her.[31] When we arrived at the Grotto, we all took out our Rosaries and knelt to pray.[32] Scarcely had I finished the first decade when I saw the same Lady. As soon as I saw the vision, I threw some holy water on her, telling her that if

[25] Ravier grouped three rough draft accounts together that come from a manuscript that he called Liasse Déal. The group includes an account of the apparitions (called GLA), an account of visits to Father Peyramale and the police interrogations (GLB) and a draft of the *Carnet à la Reine du Ciel et de la Terre* (GLC). The preceding lines come from GLA.

[26] "I told them no", meant: "No, she does not mean us harm." Although she had been seized with fear, Bernadette knew the Holy Virgin did not want to harm her.

[27] Unidentified woman (quoted in ESB).

[28] GLA (quoted in ESB).

[29] Father Gondrand (quoted in ESB).

[30] *Journal* (quoted in ESB).

[31] Father Gondrand (quoted in ESB).

[32] GLA (quoted in ESB).

she came from God to stay, but if not to go away. The more I sprinkled her with holy water, the more she smiled and bowed her head, and the more she gestured to me. So then, completely overcome with fear, I hurriedly splashed her until my bottle was empty. Then I continued to pray my Rosary, and when I finished, she disappeared, and we left to go to Vespers.[33] She did not speak to me until the third time.[34]

The third time was the following Thursday. When I arrived at the Grotto, I again began with a few *Ave Marias*. I saw the same vision.[35] I was with some adults who had advised me to take paper and ink and say to her: "If you have something to say to me, would you be kind enough to write it down?" I said those very words to the Lady. She began to smile, and she told me that it was not necessary to write down what she had to tell me.[36] She asked me if I would have the grace to return to the Grotto for fifteen days[37] and I said yes. She asked me to go tell the priests that they should have a chapel built there. She also asked

---

[33] *Journal* (quoted in ESB).

[34] Unidentified woman (quoted in ESB).

[35] *Journal* (quoted in ESB).

[36] GLA (quoted in ESB).

[37] The Lady specified fifteen days, or *quinze jours* in French. *Quinze jours* can be translated in English to mean two weeks. It should be noted, however, that the French count two weeks from one Thursday, for example, to the second Thursday that follows, which is literally fifteen days. This was the third apparition; there would be fifteen more apparitions, but they did not occur every day. Bernadette returned to the Grotto more than fifteen times after this apparition; however, the Holy Virgin appeared to her exactly fifteen times after making this request. The Holy Virgin used the respectful form of "you" (*vous*), contrary to what one would expect. Bernadette was only fourteen years old and she was poor. No one had ever addressed her as *vous* before, and she was not accustomed to being treated with such dignity and respect.

me to go drink from the spring and wash there; since I did not see a spring, I started toward the Gave.[38] She said that that was not the right place and she pointed to another place, showing me the spring under the Grotto. I went to the place she showed me, but all I saw was a tiny bit of muddy water. There was so little of it that I was hardly able to get any of it in my hands. Nevertheless, I obeyed and started digging with my hands. I tried to drink it, but it was so dirty that the first three times it came back up. On the fourth try, I was able to drink a little of it.[39] She asked me, for the sake of sinners, would I mind eating some grass that was in the same place where I drank. She asked that only once; I do not know why. She said, "Would you be willing[40] to kiss the ground for the sake of sinners? Would you be willing to crawl on your knees, for the sake of sinners? Penance! Penance! Penance!"[41] She asked me to pray for the conversion of sinners. This merciful Queen looked sad when she told me to pray for sinners.[42] She repeated these same words to me several times. She also told me that she did not promise to make me happy in this world, but

[38] *Journal* (quoted in ESB). When Bernadette wrote or spoke about the third apparition, she often summed up many of the details of the apparitions that followed.

[39] GLC (quoted in ESB).

[40] The tone of this request is difficult to translate because the Holy Virgin expressed a number of things simultaneously. It was both a polite request and a certainty that Bernadette would say yes. At the same time, the Holy Virgin knew these actions would normally be repugnant. In essence, she was saying to Bernadette, "It will not bother you too much to do these unpleasant things for the sake of sinners, will it?"

[41] GLA (quoted in ESB).

[42] Unidentified man (quoted in ESB).

in the next.[43] I saw her every day during the next fifteen days except on a Monday and a Friday.[44]

The third time, I went to see Monsieur le Curé[45] to tell him that the Lady had asked me to go tell the priests to have a chapel built at the Grotto and that people should come there in procession. He looked at me for a moment and then he said to me in a rather stern tone: "Who is this Lady?" I answered that I did not know. Then he instructed me to ask her name and to come back and tell him. The next day when I arrived at the Grotto, after having recited the Rosary, I told her that Monsieur le Curé would like to know her name, but she only smiled. When I went back to town, I went to see Monsieur le Curé and I told him that I had done what he had asked me to do, but that her only response was a smile. He said that she was making fun of me and I would do well not to go back again; however, I could not keep myself from going back. I returned for fifteen days and each time I asked her who she was, which always made her smile.[46] During the course of these fifteen days, this loving Mother told me three secrets that she forbade me to share with anyone. Thus far, I have been faithful.[47] At the end of the fifteen days, I asked her name three times in a row, and it was only when I dared to ask a fourth time that she told me.[48] Until that moment, her two arms had been extended, but now she folded her hands together

[43] GLA (quoted in ESB).

[44] Father Bouin (quoted in ESB). Bernadette was very troubled when the Holy Virgin did not appear on these two days. She was afraid of having done something to offend her.

[45] *Monsieur le Curé* was Father Marie-Dominique Peyramale, the pastor of Bernadette's parish church.

[46] GLB (quoted in ESB).

[47] Father Gondrand (quoted in ESB).

[48] GLB (quoted in ESB).

at her breast, and, raising her eyes to heaven, she said: "I am the Immaculate Conception." [49] These were the last words she said to me. [50] So once again I went to Monsieur le Curé to tell him that she had said she was the Immaculate Conception. He asked me if I were absolutely sure and I said yes. In fact, in order to be sure not to forget these words, I had repeated them to myself the entire way back.

Bernadette is Interrogated by the Civil Authorities

On the first Sunday after the fifteen days, as I was leaving the church, a police officer took me by the hood and ordered me to follow him. I followed him and as we were walking, he told me that they were going to show me the prison. I listened in silence and we soon arrived at the Police Commissioner's office. [51] He had me go in a room alone with him. He gave me a chair and I sat down. Then he took some paper and told me to tell him what had happened at the Grotto and I did so. After writing a few lines as I had dictated them to him, he wrote down other things that were completely foreign to me. Then he said that he was going to read it aloud to see if he had made any mistakes, so I listened attentively, but scarcely had he read a few lines when there were already mistakes. I spoke up in a very forthright way: "Monsieur, that is not what I said." He became angry and he kept insisting "yes I had" and I kept repeating "no I had not". These arguments lasted a few minutes and when he saw that he was mistaken and that I would persist in

[49] Unidentified man (quoted in ESB).
[50] GLC (quoted in ESB).
[51] Dominique Jacomet was the Police Commissioner.

saying that I had not said what he said I had said, he would go a little further down his notes and then begin reading what I had never said, and I would keep maintaining that that was not how it had happened. We kept going through this same routine for about an hour and a half. Now and then I heard people kicking the doors and the windows and voices of men who were shouting: "If you don't let her leave, we will kick the door in."

When they finally let me leave, the Police Commissioner walked me to the door. When he opened it, there was my father who was waiting for me impatiently, along with a crowd of other people who had followed me from the church. That was the first time I was forced to appear before those gentlemen.

The second time was at the office of the Imperial Prosecutor.[52] He sent the Police Commissioner that very week; he told me to be at the office of the Imperial Prosecutor at six o'clock. My mother and I went there together and he asked me what had happened at the Grotto. I told him everything and he wrote it down. Then he read it back to me the same way that the Police Commissioner had done; in other words, he wrote down a lot of things that I had not said. So I said: "Monsieur, I did not say that to you." He insisted that I had, and the only reply I made was "no." Finally, after going back and forth like this for quite a while, he would admit that he was mistaken. He would begin reading again, but always making new errors, saying that he had the papers from the office of the police and that they were different from what I was saying now. I told him that I had told exactly the same story before and if the Police Commissioner had made mistakes, that was his problem. So he

---

[52] The Imperial Prosecutor was Vital Dutour.

told his wife to send for the Police Commissioner and an officer to take me to prison. My poor mother, who was looking back and forth from me to him, had already started to cry a little. When she heard that they were going to put me in prison, she burst into tears. I tried to console her, saying: "You are very good to cry because they are going to put me in prison, since I have done nothing wrong to anyone." When he was just about to let us leave, he finally offered us chairs. My mother, who was trembling, accepted one because we had been standing during the whole two hours that we were there. As for me, I thanked Monsieur le Procureur, and then I sat down on the floor tailor fashion.[53] There were some men who were looking in and when they saw how long we were staying in there, they began kicking the door. The police officer was there, but he had completely lost control of the situation. Every now and then, the Imperial Prosecutor would go to the window and ask everyone to calm down, but they said they would not stop until we were allowed to leave. At that point, he decided to send us away, saying that he was busy and the whole affair would have to wait until the following day.[54]

[53] Tailors sat cross-legged on the floor. Bernadette preferred to sit on the floor rather than accept a chair from Dutour.

[54] GLB (quoted in ESB).

CHAPTER 2

A Holy Life: The Private Notes of
Saint Bernadette of Lourdes

Saint Bernadette collected thoughts on the spiritual life from a number of sources and carefully copied them down in a small notebook, interspersing them with her own prayers and thoughts. This tiny anthology of Private Notes [1] *is the most precious document from Bernadette's writings, for it offers us a glimpse into the spiritual life of "the most secret of saints". The visionary who was blessed with so many apparitions of the Holy Virgin Mary had great difficulty expressing her spiritual state, even with her spiritual director, Father Douce. The notes that were dear to Bernadette allow us to enter into the spiritual life of this humble nun, this great saint, by meditating on the thoughts that sustained her, instructed her and encouraged her.*

Although most entries are not original, her choices, indeed even her misquotes, are a reflection of her spiritual life. The Private Notes *include the following:*

1. *Extracts from spiritual books.*
2. *Bernadette's own spontaneous prayers and thoughts.*
3. *Extracts from the journal of annual retreats (1860–1870) by Father Pierre Olivaint, S.J.* [2]

---

[1] *Carnet de notes intimes.*

[2] The abbreviation OJR in these footnotes refers to Father Olivaint's *Journal de Retraite* (Retreat Journal).

4. *Her notes from a retreat given by the Reverend Father
    Sécail, S.J., in October 1873. (During this retreat Father
    Douce, chaplain of the Convent of Saint-Gildard, was her
    confessor and spiritual director. Notes she made about his
    advice to her reveal much about her spiritual life.)*
5. *A text copied from an image of the Holy Virgin.*
6. *Notes taken during a retreat given by Father Candeloup,
    S.J., in September 1874, the advice given to her by Father
    Douce in confession during this retreat and her resolutions.*
7. *Thoughts on holiness and on the Rule of the Congregation.*

1873

From this moment on, anything concerning me is no longer of any interest to me. I must belong entirely to God,
and God alone. Never to myself.

Mary sacrificed all to God; she needed him alone. From
this day forward, I shall follow her example: the Lord alone
will be my portion. Why have I come here if not to love
Our Lord with all my heart. As proof of my love for him,
I must suffer and generously sacrifice everything to him, as
Mary did. Courage, my soul, through prayer we can do all
that is asked of us. The heart of Jesus is there: let us knock.

O Divine Jesus, impress on my heart a disposition like
that of a certain man who loved your cross so much that he
used to say if after serving you for a hundred years his only
recompense were the grace to suffer one hour for love of
you, he would believe all his service too well rewarded.

O Virtue! How rarely we see you, yet how real you are![3]

O Jesus and Mary, let my entire consolation in this world be to love you and to suffer for sinners.

O my Jesus, teach me to understand the holy Jealousy of heavenly Love! Free me from earthly attachments and raise all my affections up to you. May my crucified heart be forever lost in your own and hidden away in the mysterious wound made by the spear.

O Jesus, I would rather die a thousand deaths than be unfaithful to you!

O Immaculate Mary! O glorious Saint Joseph! And you, Saint John, beloved disciple of the Divine Heart, teach me the great science of love! May it draw me powerfully! May I soar at last, may I take flight and hasten to lose myself, unite myself and disappear with you in the adorable[4] heart of Jesus, and Jesus Crucified, the divine heart of Charity, purity, self-denial and perfect submission.

I must die to myself continually and accept trials without complaining. I work, I suffer and I love with no other witness

[3] From the words "O Divine Jesus" to "how real you are", *Souffrances de Notre-Seigneur Jésus-Christ* (The suffering of our Lord Jesus Christ), written in Portuguese around 1580 by Fr. Thomas de Jésus and translated into French by Fr. Alleaume in 1692. The original text said "Truth", not "Virtue".

[4] Bernadette made frequent use of the qualifier "adorable" in its religious meaning of "worthy of adoration". Although the three-word expression is clearer to English readers, it detracts from the rhythm of the sentence and places excessive emphasis on the qualifier, weakening the impact of the substantive.

than his heart.[5] Anyone who is not prepared to suffer all for the Beloved and to do his will in all things is not worthy of the sweet name of Friend, for here below, Love without suffering does not exist.

It is in loving the cross that one discovers his heart, for divine Love does not exist without suffering.[6]

I shall spend every moment loving. One who loves does not notice her trials; or perhaps more accurately, she is able to love them.

Why must we suffer? Because here below pure Love cannot exist without suffering. O Jesus, Jesus, I no longer feel my cross when I think of yours.[7]

O my soul, imitate Jesus faithfully: he is gentle and humble of heart. Those who are humble of heart will be glorified. How beautiful the heavenly crown will be for those who are genuinely humble despite outward humiliations, those who follow the humility of the Savior in every way.[8]

O Mary, my gentle Mother, here I am, your child who can bear no more. See my needs and above all my spiritual distress. Have pity on me; grant that one day I may be with you in Heaven.

[5] The quotation beginning with the words "I must die to myself" and ending with the words "than his heart" is found on the back of an image of the Sacred Heart.

[6] These lines rhyme in the original French, suggesting that it is not original. The source remains unidentified.

[7] From "Why must we" to "I think of yours", extract from a text on both sides of an image representing "Mary, the Crucifix, the Soul".

[8] From "O my soul" to "in every way", Thomas de Jésus.

I shall do everything for Heaven, my true home. There I shall find my Mother in all the splendor of her glory. I shall delight with her in the joy of Jesus himself in perfect safety.

O Mary, my good Mother, help me follow your example to be generous in every sacrifice Our Lord may ask of me during my life.

O my Mother, offer me to Jesus. Take my heart and unite it with the heart of my Jesus.

Jesus came on earth to be my model. I want to follow him and walk generously in his footsteps.

Divine Heart of my Jesus, grant that I may love you always, and always more.[9]

O Mary, receive my heart as an expiatory victim for my offenses; may it be broken with sadness.

O my Mother, to you I sacrifice all other attachments so that my heart may belong entirely to you and to my Jesus.

O my Mother, come to my aid; grant me the grace of dying to myself so I will no longer live save in my sweet Jesus and for my Jesus.

[9] From "Divine Heart" to "always more", paraphrase from a text of the Garde d'Honneur.

I want to follow you and be like you, O my Jesus; I would rather be crucified with you than enjoy all the pleasures of this world without you.[10]

My sweet Jesus, give me a great love for the cross, and if I do not die at the hands of others as you did, may I die by the intensity of my love.[11]

O my Jesus, help me to love you; love me, and then crucify me as much as you please.[12]

Jesus, my God, I love you above all things.

Dear gentle Jesus, be not my judge, but my Savior.[13]

I want to sacrifice all and suffer without complaining since my Jesus keeps me from all fear.[14]

Love overcomes, love delights,
Those who love the Sacred Heart rejoice.[15]

[10] From "I want to follow" to "without you", Thomas de Jésus.

[11] From "if I do not die" to "the intensity of my love", Thomas de Jésus.

[12] From "love me" to "you please", paraphrase from Thomas de Jésus.

[13] From "Dear gentle Jesus" to "my Savior", prayer attributed to Saint Jerome Emilien.

[14] From "I want to sacrifice" to "all fear", quote from St. Margaret Mary Alacoque that St. Bernadette changed to a great extent. It is taken from *La Vie de la Bienheureuse Marguerite-Marie, Religieuse de la Visitation Sainte-Marie* (The life of Blessed Margaret Mary, Sister of the Visitation of Holy Mary), by Father Croiset of the Company of Jesus.

[15] From "Love overcomes" to "Heart rejoice", *Vie de la Bienheureuse Marguerite-Marie.*

Those who are humble of heart will be glorified. How beautiful the heavenly crown will be for those who are genuinely humble despite outward humiliations, those who follow the humility of the Savior in every way.[16]

O my beloved Jesus, the sighs of my heart rise up to you alone.

Margaret Mary Alacoque said:[17] "I wanted no one to remember me save to scorn me, humble me and insult me; for indeed, that is all I deserved." [18]

O Jesus, you who were forsaken have become the refuge of forsaken souls. Your love teaches me that I must gain the strength I need to endure being abandoned by seeing how you were abandoned. I am persuaded that the most terrible abandonment I could experience would be to have no part in yours. By your death, you gave me life; you delivered me from the suffering I deserved by suffering in my place. Because of what you endured on the cross, our Heavenly Father will not desert me. He is never closer to me through his mercy than when I am most united with you in your abandonment.

O Jesus, light of my soul, enlighten me during times of tribulation; and since these trials are useful to me, pay no heed to my fears or my weakness.

[16] Repeated text. On a few occasions, Bernadette repeated a quote.

[17] "*M. M. Victim*" in the original text. Margaret Mary Alacoque was canonized in 1920.

[18] From "I wanted" to "I deserved", *Vie de la Bienheureuse Marguerite-Marie*.

O my God, I do not ask you to keep me from suffering, but to be with me in affliction. Teach me to seek you as my only comforter; sustain my faith; strengthen my hope; purify my love. Grant me the grace to recognize your hand in the midst of suffering and to want no other comforter than you.[19]

Humble me as much as you want. Console me only when it may help me accept suffering and persevere until death. Since the graces I ask are the fruits of your abandonment, bring virtue out of my weakness and glorify yourself in my misery, O my Jesus, the only refuge of my soul.

O Most Holy Mother of my Jesus, you who saw and felt the extreme desolation of your dear Son, help me in my own time of desolation.

And you, saints of Heaven who have passed through this trial, have pity on those who are suffering it now and pray that I be given the grace to be faithful until death.[20]

I turn to you, O Father of mercy! Receive me, O God of all consolation! Sustain me with your grace and grant that so much suffering and so much love may not be in vain.[21]

Jesus gives all to those who surrender all.

---

[19] Variation: instead of "no other comforter than you", the original text reads "no other consolation than that which comes from you".

[20] From "O Jesus, you who were forsaken" to "until death", Thomas de Jésus, "'Interview' with Jesus Christ abandoned by his Father".

[21] From "I turn to you" to "not be in vain", Thomas de Jésus.

The more obstacles there are to my love, the stronger it becomes. It is my one and only possession. Even if I were tormented day and night, no one could take it from my soul. The more I suffer, the more I will draw close to his heart.[22]

A righteous person is a victim and his life a continual sacrifice. For love of Jesus, I will fight against my own desires even in the most insignificant matters.

Watch over me, Father, so that everything I do may be with the intention of pleasing Jesus.

O most merciful heart of my Jesus, accept each of my tears, every cry of pain, as a plea for those who suffer, for those who weep, for those who forget you.

O Mary, O Mother of sorrows! At the foot of the cross, you became our Mother. I am the child of your sorrow, the child of Calvary.[23]

O most loveable Jesus, the sighs of my heart rise up to you.

My Jesus, I suffer and I love you ...

I suffer. My comforter, my moans rise up to you without ceasing. It is in your most Adorable heart that I shed

[22] From "The more obstacles" to "to his heart", *Vie et Oeuvres de la Bienheureuse Marguerite-Marie Alacoque* (The life and works of Blessed Margaret Mary Alacoque), Paray-le-Monial. "Canticle to the Sacred Heart", composed by Margaret Mary Alacoque. Bernadette changed the text: the original reads "The more I suffer, the more he will unite me to his heart."
[23] From "O Mary" to "child of Calvary", *Suite des Entretiens spirituels*, by Father de Ravignan.

my tears. It is to your heart that I confide my sighs and my anguish. I unite my sufferings with yours. My Jesus, sanctify them through this holy union. Let this union make them sweeter and lighter and let me grow in love.

My divine spouse has made me desire a humble and hidden life. Jesus has often told me that I will not die until I have sacrificed all to him. And to convince me, he has often told me that when it is over, at the hour of death, he alone, Jesus crucified, will console me. I will carry only him, my faithful friend, with me to my grave. It is madness to attach myself to anything other than him.

A Poor Beggar's Prayer to Jesus.

O Jesus, grant me, I pray, the bread of humility,
the bread of obedience,
the bread of charity,
the bread of strength to break my will and make it conform
    to yours,
the bread of interior mortification,
the bread of detachment,
the bread of patience to endure the pain my heart suffers.
    O Jesus, you want me crucified, *fiat,*
the bread of strength to suffer well,
the bread of seeing only you in everything, at every moment,
Jesus, Mary, the Cross, I want no other friends than these.

If I had to remake my character entirely, struggle endlessly against my own inclinations and destroy them, or even tear my own heart out, all this I would do to be worthy of serving you. I am entirely persuaded that the miracle you worked to reward the faith of our holy patron is but a shadow of the glorious resurrection you will deign to grant me if I am faithful to my vocation.[24]

The faithful soul obeys God's will for the Church. Her spouse wants her to be perfect in every way, doing all with faith and charity. In this way, the Father will be the guiding principle for her actions; the Son, the source of her light; and the Holy Spirit the source of her love.

Union, intimate union with Jesus, heart to heart with Jesus like Saint John, in purity and in love.[25]

O Jesus, keep me as your own.

My hope is in you, Lord. Be my refuge, for you are my strength. . . . Into your hands, Lord, I commend my spirit. You have redeemed me, Lord, God of Truth.[26]

I was nothing, yet out of this nothingness Jesus has made something wondrous. I dare to say this for through Holy Communion I become one with God. Jesus gives me his heart; my heart is joined with his. I am the spouse of Jesus, the friend of Jesus, in other words, another Jesus. So I must[27]

---

[24] From "If I had to remake" to "my vocation", *Manuel de piété* (Handbook of piety) of the Sisters of Nevers (Nevers, 1844). Meditations for the Feast of St. Martha, p. 313. Bernadette omitted three words: "To be worthy of serving you *in the poor* . . ."

[25] From "Union, intimate union" to "in love", OJR, p. 57.

[26] From "Into your hands" to "God of truth", translation of the *In Manus tuas*. As in many religious communities, it was customary in the Congregation of Nevers to recite this prayer (which is part of Compline) before going to bed.

[27] OJR, p. 57.

live through Jesus, and my death must resemble the death of Jesus himself. How sublime is our death if we are faithful!

Above all, I must be attached to no one but Jesus Christ. I ask him for his light, his strength, his divine life. I must strive for a holy death in him and with him. I am a Religious, thus I have made a profession of perfection.

The Christian life does indeed mean battles and trials, but it is also means consolations.[28] And though I must leave Tabor and climb to Calvary, one day I will leave Calvary with Jesus and return to Tabor. A foretaste of Heaven awaits me there. My soul follows but one path: from Golgotha to Tabor. It leaves Golgotha to seek strength and courage at Tabor. Life is such a ladder.

I must work with all my strength to destroy self-love and self-interest.[29]

Jesus does not want us to be attached to possessions, to human honors, to creatures. He asks humility. But his love and his generosity make this detachment less difficult and less cruel to our nature. Nothing else matters to me anymore, nothing has any value for me but Jesus, no place, no thing, no person, no idea, no feeling, no honor, no suffering, nothing that can turn me away from Jesus. For me, Jesus himself is my honor, my delight, my heart, my spirit, he whom I love, what I love, my home, Heaven here on

[28] Bernadette transposed texts of the OJR to adapt to the situation of a woman and a Religious. For example, where Father Olivaint said "priest" or "Mass", Bernadette said "Religious" or "Communion". (OJR pp. 87, 60, 61).

[29] From "The Christian life" to "self-interest", OJR, pp. 71, 79. Cf. *L'Echelle mystique* (The mystical ladder) (ESB no. 213, pp. 489–90).

earth. Jesus is my treasure and my love and Jesus crucified is my only happiness.

Jesus, keep me under the standard of your cross. May the crucifix not be just something I wear, something I look at, but let it be alive in my heart. Let me be transformed into a living crucifixion, in union with you through the Eucharist. By meditating on your life and the most intimate feelings of your heart, let me draw souls to you from high on this cross where your love holds me forever.

Have mercy. Protect us from the temptations of the Demon and the illusions those temptations carry with them. Protect us from the kind of passion and sensuality that makes us disloyal and unfaithful to God.[30]

New examination of conscience. Regret for having lacked charity toward Jesus so often, for having stifled in myself the charity of Jesus Christ himself so often.
So many people say that Father Villefort is overflowing with charity. How I would like to be like that.

Resolution: In the future, be more charitable toward the poor (both the materially poor and the spiritually poor).[31]

Preparation for Holy Communion.
The best preparation is meditation. I do that so badly!

[30] From "Jesus does not want" to "unfaithful to God", OJR, pp. 49–50. The sentence "Jesus is my treasure and my love and Jesus crucified is my only happiness" was added by Bernadette.
[31] From "New examination" to "spiritually poor", OJR, pp. 47–48.

Renew and strengthen the resolutions I have made in this regard.[32]

But I am so exhausted in the morning. Remind myself of the temptation Father Avila experienced one day when he was on his way to celebrate Mass. He hesitated because he was so weary. Our Lord appeared to him, showing him the wound on his heart and reminding him that weariness had not prevented him from going all the way to Calvary. Courage! I must learn how to persevere also.

After all, if I am tired, even if I am exhausted, I can rest in the heart of Jesus.

Take every opportunity to poor oil and wine on wounds as Jesus did, not vinegar, and without regard to person. Or like Jesus, reach out to the poorest, to those who are suffering most, to the most humble, the most abandoned. In the future, be more charitable to others, recognize both their physical and spiritual poverty.[33]

For love of Jesus and to glorify God, I will generously accept privations, suffering and mortifications as Jesus and Mary did.

Everything is the Father's will: homeland, fortune, happiness, work, food, life, Jesus' death. Let his will be mine.

My soul, rejoice that you resemble Jesus a little in that you are hidden behind lowliness!

[32] From "Preparation" to "in this regard", OJR, pp. 60–61.

[33] From "But I am so exhausted" to "spiritual poverty", OJR, pp. 60, 61, 48. Bernadette replaced the words "heart of the Master" with "heart of Jesus" and added "to the poorest".

May I let Jesus lead me more easily. May I be ready to accept everything, even mortification, powerlessness, living in darkness, being hidden like Jesus in a dark prison. If I let it, this prison or whatever this mortification may be will be the heart of Mary for me.

Jesus Christ at his birth: I contemplate him there with Mary and Joseph. What conditions, though! Lying in a manger where animals feed! Humiliation, privation, suffering.

For the greater glory of God, the important thing is not to do many things, but to do all things well.

What does it profit a man to gain the universe if he loses his soul? A terrible thought, but profoundly true! As Saint Ignatius said: How insignificant earth seems to me when I consider Heaven.[34]

A good Religious should ask God for:

More humility than mortifications,
More patience than suffering,
More willingness than works,
More love than actions,
More self-denial than orders,
More results than words,
More zeal for holiness than for health.[35]

---

[34] From "For love of Jesus" to "when I consider Heaven", OJR, pp. 126–28.
[35] Petit livre des novices (Little book for novices) by the author of the book for Superiors and Paillettes d'Or (Grains of gold) (Aubanel, Avignon, 1873), p. 115.

The cross

O my God, if I cannot shed my blood and give my life for you, may I at least die to all that displeases you: sin, earthly desires, desires of the flesh, the world and myself. Cross of my Savior, holy cross, cross worthy of adoration, in you alone are my strength, my hope and my joy. You are the tree of life, the mysterious ladder that unites earth to Heaven, the altar on which I want to sacrifice myself by dying with Jesus.

Unlimited self-denial. Love for and fidelity to Jesus, my Spouse, until death.

The heart of Jesus with all its treasures is my portion. I shall live and die there in peace, even in the midst of suffering.

My Jesus, fill my heart with so much love that one day it will break just to be with you. My Jesus, you know I have placed you as a seal on my heart. Remain there always.

Retreat given by Reverend Father Sécail in 1873[36]

Tuesday 9:00 A.M.

(1) God is my Creator; (2) my Savior; (3) my Sanctifier. I belong to God, therefore he is absolute master of my body,

---

[36] Fr. Sécail, S.J., was the speaker at the retreat. Bernadette collected various thoughts from the retreat, but she intertwined them with personal reflections and prayers. Subject headings are added and are not found in the *Private Notes*.

my soul and my actions. He wants me to sacrifice my will to him at every moment and in everything. In the hands of my superiors, I should be like a dead person, or more accurately like a staff. Never mind if they make mistakes. I know that I will never be wrong if I obey with a spirit of faith.

My crown in Heaven should shine with innocence and its flowers should be as radiant as the sun. Sacrifices are the flowers Jesus and Mary chose.

I must be a victim; that is to say, I should live sacrificially every day as Jesus and Mary did.

On detachment

Saint Ignatius does not insist that we be indifferent, but that we *try to become* indifferent. My heart is made for God and he is jealous. I want it to be entirely his. I will become a saint if I am humble, docile and generous.

On the poverty of Jesus Christ

Poverty should not just be difficult, but crucifying. Jesus chose the most humble things to satisfy his needs, such as hay to soothe his frail and delicate body. If he ever had any preference, it was always for suffering; unlike him, I choose comfort and pleasure. With the help of your grace, starting today, that is over. I want to walk in your footsteps, suffer, conquer my weaknesses and die to all that is not you, in order to live for Jesus, with Jesus and in Jesus. In this way, I shall belong entirely to Jesus. How sweet it will be to die in this way with Jesus!

On temptation

Holy Scripture tells us that whoever gives in to temptation will perish. Never fear temptation: it is useful and necessary to us. I must arm myself with prayer and have complete trust in Our Lord and great mistrust of myself. I must face every trial with profound humility and blind, simple, happy obedience.

Jesus crucified is my model. I must work tirelessly to be like him. I should no longer allow myself to be sad about anything other than offending him or having nothing to suffer for him, for love of him.

What was mine no longer belongs to me. I have given all to Jesus.

Resolution: Energy to break my will even in the most insignificant things. Pause twice a day and make reparations for the time I have lost.

Detachment from creatures and things. Watch over my emotions. Listen to Jesus who says to me so often: "My daughter, give me your heart. I want it entirely to myself."

Communal life, holy life.

The more I contemplate God, the more God looks on me. The more I pray to him, the more he thinks of me too.[37]

---

[37] From "The more I contemplate" to "looks on me", quote by St. Bernard, borrowed from the *Directoir* ... p. 19. (Cf. similar thoughts are also found in the *Oeuvres du P. de Laveyne*, by Fr. Bouix, 1871, chap. XII, p. 69.)

Father Douce[38]: You must carry your cross hidden in your heart as Mary did.

Resolution: I will be joyful when I go to the parlor, even if my heart is full of sadness.

I shall say to God: Yes, I will go there on the condition that you free a soul from Purgatory or convert a sinner.

Father Douce: Place yourself in the heart of Mary and remain there. Make it your home on earth.

O my Mother, it is to your heart that I come to lay down the anguish of my heart; it is there that I draw strength and courage.

Do not be afraid to carry the cross, even naked.

The more I give to Jesus, the more he will give me. For love of Jesus, I must overcome my weakness or die.[39]

Consider Saint John the Baptist on the banks of the Jordan[40]

How austere and implacable he is! Jesus has not yet come, but look how Saint John prepares the way for him; how he inspires contrition through repentance; how he heralds the coming of Jesus! How he leads to Jesus! How he decreases

[38] Bernadette noted the advice given to her by Father Douce, Chaplain of Saint-Gildard after confession during the retreat.

[39] Bernadette wove resolutions together with advice, just as she combined personal reflections and pious thoughts with notes from the lecture. This notebook was intended for her alone.

[40] She again began to quote from OJR.

before Jesus! *Debeo a te baptizari*[41] ... See how humble and obedient he is before Jesus: *Sic nos decet implere omnem justitiam*,[42] Jesus said, *Omnem*[43] ... As Savior, by atoning for sins; as a sinner, by humbling himself and taking their place; as the Just One, by purifying himself again ... *Omnem*, for Saint John the Baptist, as herald, by paying homage to his mission; as a servant, by obeying this Master who pays him homage.

Yet another reason for Saint John the Baptist to exclaim: "*Oportet illum crescere, me autem minui.*"[44] I must do like him for I am still so very human ... too inflexible like Saint John the Baptist.

I absolutely must do this so that God may be more glorified, so that my vocation will be better fulfilled, so that his grace will not be wasted in me, so that I may atone for the past and assure the future. But increase how, and diminish how? For Jesus to increase, I must decrease. His presence increases in proportion to how much I decrease. If I do not, I prevent him from increasing.

[41] *Debeo a te baptizari*: "I need to be baptized by you." When Jesus asked John to baptize him, John responded: "I need to be baptized by you, and do you come to me?"

[42] *Sic nos decet implere omnem justitiam*: "Let it be so now; for it is proper for us in this way to fulfill all righteousness." According to *Harper's Biblical Commentary*, ed. James L. Mays (San Francisco: Harper and Row, 1988), p. 953, *omnem justitiam*, or "a fulfillment of all righteousness" is "an obscure phrase. It very probably refers to Jesus' identification of himself, as he comes to be baptized, as a devout Jew who observes the law and the practices associated with good Jewish life."

[43] *Omnem*: "all".

[44] *Oportet illum crescere, me autem minui*: "He must increase. I must decrease" (Jn 4:30).

Why is he so little in me? It is because I am not little enough, not humble enough. Therefore may I become more humble, may I humble myself, and Jesus will increase.

Grow, Jesus, grow in me, in my heart, in my spirit, my imagination, my senses, by your modesty, your purity, your humility, your zeal, your love. Grow with your grace, your light, your peace. Grow despite my resistance, my pride. Grow until you reach the fullness of human perfection. Grow as you did at Nazareth before God and before men, for the glory of your Father.[45]

Ad majorem Dei gloriam[46]

We are tempted by pride to the same degree that we experience God's glory, God's love, humility and poverty. To keep from preferring pleasure and honor, we must care about ourselves too much to seek these things.

When we are tempted to break God's law, we must love ourselves too much to risk committing a venial sin. We must love ourselves too much to risk committing a mortal sin.

Put faith into practice by thinking on these four truths:

God is always present.
Nothing happens without his permission or outside of his will.

[45] From "Consider Saint John the Baptist" to "the glory of your Father", OJR, pp. 132–33.

[46] *Ad majorem Dei gloriam*: "To the greater glory of God" (often abbreviated A.M.D.G., as Bernadette has done elsewhere).

Anything we do to others we do to him.
All kindness and goodness are in him.

Live faith with these truths:

Drive out all sin.
Console all grief.
Cast away all listlessness.
Enrich the soul with the life of grace.[47] One day God will
  say about us: *quoniam bene.*[48]

How? union with Jesus and Mary.

Baptism of Jesus Christ

Jesus Christ leaves his mother. *Sciebat.*[49] She is resigned to
it, or perhaps it is more accurate to say that she sends him,
follows him in her heart and soon she is with him again.
Jesus knows how to sacrifice the bonds of nature without
wounding his mother's heart. Look at him going toward
the Jordan. He has waited so long for the moment when
he would begin his mission! Nevertheless, he does not hurry.
He has an extraordinary kind of self-control. His Father's

[47] From "We are tempted" to "life of grace", OJR, pp. 136–37. Bernadette made two important changes: after "humility" she added "poverty",
and she replaced "abundance of virtues" with "the life of grace".

[48] *Quoniam bene*: "You have done well."

[49] *Sciebat*: "Did you not know", Lk 2:49. Joseph and Mary have taken the
twelve-year-old Jesus to Jerusalem for the festival of Passover. On the way
home, they realize that he is missing and when they return to Jerusalem they
find him teaching in the temple. When Mary asks him why he has done
this, he replies: "Why were you searching for me? Did you not know that I
must be in my Father's house?"

will governs everything. His only thought is to do his Father's will.

His first apostolic steps, so gentle and so solemn, draw people and inspire respect. And here I am so hurried and so inflexible! How many souls are frightened away by the thought of submitting to God's will!

Why does God ask for this union and submission to his will? Because it is absolutely just, loveable, superior to everything, so much so that there is no plausible reason ever to reject it. God's will is the only sure rule of conduct.

However good our intentions may be, it is always wrong to go against God's will; it is always an illusion and a mistake.

We need never fear being deceived by illusion if we follow the will of God because it is the true secret to the highest perfection. It is the sure means of glorifying God in all things. *Ad majorem Dei gloriam!* It is not important to do many things or extraordinary things; it is only important to do God's will because the entire Gospel is in that, the entire life of Our Lord. This practice is certain help in times of darkness, for God can never deceive us.

I know in whom I have put my trust. I choose what God wills, as he wills it, because he wills it because this is the secret of peace and happiness. If we do this, it can be said of us, as of Jesus: "*Bene omnia fecit.*" [50] And at every instant we ourselves can say, as God said after the creation:

[50] *Bene omnia fecit*: "He has done all things well" (Mk 7:37).

"*Et vidit quod esset bonum*," [51] because a good judgment awaits us after death.[52]

From now on, may I put his will above all else: home-land, fortune, happiness, food, life. Jesus' sole desire was to do his Father's will. Let it also be mine. And why should I complain about trials? Without trials, I shall never be detached from my own desires; I shall never truly come into God's glory.

How is it possible to do this? Purity of conscience, purity of intention, pious practices, virtues in one's vocation . . .

This year, I must overcome or die. I will wage war on my own will. For the greater glory of God, it is not impor-tant to do many things, but to do them well.

Vocation

Why the rule? What does it profit a man to gain the uni-verse and lose his soul?

Obstacles:
1. Countless occupations.
2. Undisciplined zeal, like the foolish virgins.
3. Self-interest.
4. Discouragement.

---

[51] *Et vidit quod esset bonum*: "And he saw that it was good" (Gen 1:4, 10, 12, 18, 21, 25, 31).

[52] From "God will say about us" to "awaits us after death", OJR, pp. 129–32.

1. Do not just be a channel for grace, but a reservoir, an overflowing reservoir. No sooner has a channel received grace than it pours it out. A reservoir waits to be filled up and then offers grace to those who come to draw from its superabundance.
2. If you do not act wisely, you exhaust yourself in senseless work.

The private life of Jesus Christ

He was interested in one thing alone: the holy will of his Father. This is his law and his life because it is in doing God's will that his Father is glorified. It must be absolutely clear in my mind that everything consists in doing God's holy will.

But it is not enough just to do God's will. I want to love doing God's holy will more than anything in the world.

What gifts do the shepherds bring? Not gold, incense and myrrh, but milk, fruit and sheep. In other words, purity, love, true piety and sacrifice.

And the Lamb gives himself to them. Mary presents him to them. How they embrace him in their arms, in their hearts. O Mary, keep Jesus in my heart.

Humility is the secret of God's glory.

Ad majorem Dei gloriam.

Jesus in the heart of Mary: her heart is like an altar on which the victim of expiation, adoration, supplication and thanksgiving is offered

Humiliation, suffering, privation in going to Bethlehem: so many ways to glorify God. They offer every trial to God. God's love grows in them through their sacrifices, and with love, the true life.

This interior life of Jesus hidden in Mary's heart is concealed from others, but what does that matter? How easily he finds his heavenly Father in Mary! How lovingly he glorifies his Father on the altar of Mary's heart! How he rejoices in cultivating Mary's beautiful soul with his grace!

May I too have an interior life!

What does it matter if no one sees it as long as I imitate Jesus, as long as I live through Jesus and I dwell in the heart of Mary like Jesus. May I accept privations, suffering and humiliations generously as Jesus, Mary and Joseph did in order to glorify God.

This year, I must overcome or die. I will wage war on my own will. For the greater glory of God, it is not important to do many things, but to do them well.[53]

Vocation.
Why the rule?

What does it profit a man to gain the universe and lose his soul?

---

[53] Bernadette repeated these lines.

Obstacles!

1. Countless occupations.
2. Undisciplined zeal, like the foolish virgins.
3. Self-interest.
4. Discouragement.

1. Do not just be a channel for grace, but a reservoir, an overflowing reservoir. No sooner has a channel received grace than it pours it out. A reservoir waits to be filled up and then offers grace to those who come to draw from its superabundance.
2. If you do not act wisely, you exhaust yourself in senseless work.

The Private Life of Jesus: He was interested in one thing alone: the holy will of his Father. This is his law and his life because it is in doing God's will that his Father is glorified. It must be absolutely clear in my mind that everything consists in doing God's holy will.

O my Jesus, be my strength and my virtue.[54]

Meditation

1. Jesus is my model.
2. Jesus is my strength.
3. Jesus is my true consolation.

[54] From "From now on" (see p. 52 above) to "my virtue", OJR, pp. 128–29. Bernadette reversed the order of passages from Olivaint.

On the spiritual resurrection of our souls

God is jealous of my heart. He wants me to sacrifice all human affections to him generously so that he may reign there as master.

I must become a great saint. My Jesus wants it and, by virtue of my situation, it is my duty.

On the death of a righteous person

A righteous person should not fear the destruction of his body since one day he will be resurrected glorious and radiant with glory.

On the reign of Jesus

Jesus must reign:

    1.   in my heart;
    2.   in my spirit;
    3.   in my will; in other words, in my entire soul.

The Fiat[55] of Mary's child

Of all *fiats*, is this not the sweetest? Divine love unites them. Their two hearts become one to Love, to Suffer and to Obey.

---

[55] *Fiat*: "May it be done [to me according to your word]", see Lk 1:38.

No longer my will, my good Mother, but yours, which is always the will of Jesus!

MARY

Courage, my child. You have found the precious Pearl that buys the Kingdom of Heaven. To love what God wills always, to will it always, to desire it always, to do it always: this is the great secret of perfection, the key to paradise, the foretaste of the peace of the saints!

The more you unite your heart to mine, the more you will understand the truth of these words. When you no longer have any will other than God's, your heart and mine will become one and the same heart. Learn to say the *Ecce Ancilla*[56] of perfect obedience with me each day.

Whatever trials the Lord sends you, whatever sacrifices he asks of you, whatever duties he imposes on you, always have this response of love and faithfulness on your lips and in your heart: Here is your servant, O my God, ready to undertake all, to give all, to sacrifice all, to offer up all, as long as your will may be accomplished in me and on all the earth.

THE SOUL

Ah! Let it be done unto me according to your word. O my Mother, let my heart, lost in yours, have no other

[56] *Ecce Ancilla*: "I am the handmaid of the Lord", Lk 1:38.

movement, no other will, no other love than the desire of my divine Master. With my soul united to yours, let me begin here in this life[57] to glorify the Lord by this perpetual homage of perfect Submission. Yes, my God, yes . . . In everything and everywhere Yes . . .[58]

1874

A.M.G.D.

Retreat of September 7, 1874[59]

1. The most important grace to ask for during this retreat: to live more and more hidden like Jesus and Mary.

2. Detachment from others and from myself.

I will pray an *Our Father* and a *Hail Mary* every day for this intention. Resolution: fight generously against my predominant fault, sensitivity.[60] Go to the person who has hurt me and be very kind to her. Not for herself, but for the love of Our Lord.

---

[57] Words omitted here by Bernadette: "the eternal *amen* of the blessed".

[58] From "The *Fiat* of Mary's Child" to "everywhere Yes . . ." is from a text printed on an image published by C. Letaille (p. 394). Bernadette took the trouble to separate the two sections, "Mary" and further down "The Soul" as they were on the original.

[59] Retreat preached by Rev. P. Candeloup, S.J., from September 5–14.

[60] These are not notes from the retreat, but very personal notes, as are the following pages.

Advice given by Father Douce

Have no fear. Always stay very close to Our Lord, present in the Tabernacle. Be completely absorbed by devotion to him there and never let go. Pray that the Holy Virgin will keep you well hidden there. Consider this good Master. He suffers so much in silence. Even though he could easily reduce this suffering to nothingness, he does not move.

For the love of Jesus, follow his example and carry your cross hidden in your heart generously and courageously.

I have sinned. It is right that I should suffer.

From time to time, read and meditate on the chapter of the treatise on *The Royal Way of the Holy Cross*. You will find strength and courage there for the coming year.

—————— [61]

Have you been short tempered? Make an act of contrition. Humble yourself before Our Lord and go to him with confidence. It would be even better to apologize to your Sister also, but you are not obligated to do so. It is to her own disadvantage if she does not use it for her spiritual growth. She should have enough charity in her heart to consider that you have received forgiveness for your fault.

As for poverty, since you have asked permission to give and to receive, there is no need to be specific.

[61] This line in the manuscript indicates that the following advice given by Father Douce came from a different moment during the retreat.

The most important grace to ask for during this retreat: to live more and more hidden like Jesus and Mary.

Often remind yourself of this word that the Most Holy Virgin said to you: penance! penance!

You should be the first one to put it into practice. For this intention, suffer trials in silence so that Jesus and Mary may be glorified. Ask Our Lord and the Most Holy Virgin to show you the cross he wants you to carry this year. Carry it lovingly, faithfully and generously. Every evening give it back to Our Lord, who will return it to you every morning when you wake. Always receive it lovingly and generously. This cross will be your glory and your consolation.

Make an examination of conscience every month. Am I faithful in following the advice my confessor has given me in any given circumstance? Am I faithful in refraining from what he has advised me to avoid?

Let go of the past and have confidence in the future.

Grace to ask for: humility and generosity in the trials I must suffer, both mentally and physically.

Resolution: be faithful in practices of piety and in even the smallest details of our holy Rule.

Particular subject of examination: being composed in both exterior and interior trials and annoyances.

On the last day, all our virtues will be tested by fire. Only humility will be able to withstand it. Saint Ephrem.

Instruction on the spiritual resurrection of our souls

In other words, with a spirit of faith, let the goal of all our actions be to please Our Lord. The more we die on the cross, the more glorious our resurrection will be. What folly it is to pull away when Our Lord asks for our hand to nail it to the cross. From now on, the more I am crucified, the more I will rejoice ...[62]

– – – – – – – –

blank pages in the notebook

– – – – – – – –

I am the way, the truth and the life ... But to follow me, you must deny yourself, take up your cross and carry it until the last day ...

My divine Master, I have made my choice! ... I would rather suffer with You until death than rejoice even for an instant with those who insult and abandon you ... I have considered the wide way ... I have weighed the value of the passing riches of this life ... measured the length of its fleeting pleasures ... contemplated its vain happiness and its ephemeral glory. I saw bright flowers under which grow the thorns of remorse and the disappointments of sorrow.

[62] Bernadette abruptly interrupted her writing.

Thanks to your divine light, I understood it all! ... And turning my lips away from the poisoned chalice, I cried out with the Sage: Vanity of vanities; all is vanity on the earth, outside of loving God and serving him.

So I raised my eyes and I no longer saw anyone but Jesus!
Jesus alone as my Goal,
Jesus alone as my Master,
Jesus alone as my Model,
Jesus alone as my Guide,
Jesus alone as my Joy,
Jesus alone as my Wealth,
Jesus alone as my Friend!

Oh, yes, my Jesus! From now on, I want you alone to be my everything and my life. I shall follow you everywhere you go ... Come my soul, courage. Climb to Calvary behind Jesus and Mary for just one more day. And then, with Jesus and Mary: Joy, Rejoicing, Eternity!

O good Cross! O precious thorns along the way, soon your wounds will be glorious.

A Religious must live with mortification as a fish swims in water. For a Religious, there is something missing if she is not mortified. The serious practice of all her duties necessarily leads to the practice of a continual mortification at every moment. If she is not mortified, she is lacking in her duty.

What is the source of offences against the Rule and against one's vows? What is the source of the laxity of some communities? It is the fact that mortification has not been practiced or maintained. The mortification God asks of us is the precise observance of our Rule, its practices, its customs and the recommendations made by our superiors. A Sister who is truly faithful in this way practices mortification judiciously and with absolutely no danger of vanity. I believe that she could enter Heaven without passing through the fires of Purgatory!

There are many daily mortifications that a recollected and attentive soul does not let slip away. For example, we please God when we get up in winter at the appointed hour without lingering and turning over in bed.

We should control our senses. Unrestrained curiosity is an obstacle to prayer. If someone enters the house, do not look or ask who it is. As for the sense of taste, we can practice any number of mortifications without anyone noticing it. A Religious should never express a preference for a particular food. You should never hear a Religious talk about food. It shows a lack of an interior life. When she goes to meals, she should be humbled by the fact that this necessity is an act we have in common with animals, then she should remember how the saints have acted.

A Religious who allows herself to eat and drink whatever she wants will never have an interior life.

Mortification is the ABCs of perfection. Because of our nature, we are inclined to eat and drink anything that tastes good to us, but the more we give in to the body, the more it demands of us. The more we refuse it, the less it will demand of us. There are such delights in the practice of all the mortifications prescribed by our rule that a soul who has experienced them will not have enough of suffering and of crosses. Mortification has such a powerful attraction for this soul that it is never too much.

Remember, a vocation that distinguishes you from the rest of the faithful and places you in a higher position demands exceptional virtues of you. I leave you to meditate on these few words that I could call the abridged catechism of the religious state: obedience even to blind obedience, poverty even to evangelical nakedness, mortification even to crucifixion, humility even to complete prostration.

These are the sacrifices to which you are committed and that should . . .[63]

Infallible means of attaining holiness, and perfect holiness:

1.   The means God puts at our disposal: light, in other words, our rule.
2.   True willingness on our part, in other words, energetic, courageous, constant, persevering.[64]

[63] From "Remember" to "that should", borrowed from Abbot Asselin's *Discours sur la vie religieuse* (Discourse on religious life), followed by *Discours sur l'Amour de Dieu et l'oraison dominicale* (Discourse on the love of God and Dominican prayer), dedicated to Mme Louise de France, Lyon, Pelagaud, Lesne et Crozet, 1836, p. 297 (*Discours sur l'excellence de l'état religieux* ["Discourse on the excellence of religious life"]), (First edition, Paris, 1781).

[64] This last page is very different from the rest of the notebook. It is written in pencil and the handwriting suggests that Bernadette was probably quite ill. In addition, there are more misspelled words than in the rest of the notebook.

CHAPTER 3

Bernadette's Life in Lourdes
after the Apparitions
1858–1866

Bernadette's last vision of the Blessed Virgin took place on July 16, 1858.[1] In the fall of that year, she began her education gratis with the Sisters of Charity and Christian Instruction at the Hospice[2] in Lourdes. By 1860, the Sisters invited her to live with them at the Hospice, where she continued her studies. Pilgrims flocked to Lourdes from all over the world, all of them wanting to see and talk to Bernadette. These constant demands made it difficult for her to progress in her own education; however, eventually she gained the skills necessary to help the Sister who was in charge of the infirmary and she even helped teach the younger children.

Not only did Bernadette tirelessly recount the events at Massabielle for pilgrims who longed to hear her beautiful story directly from her, but she was also questioned repeatedly by Church authorities. November 17, 1858, marked the date of the first inquiry of the Episcopal Commission during which Bernadette was interrogated in Lourdes. The last official interrogation took place on December 7, 1860. On January 18, 1862, four full years after the first apparition, Monsignor Laurence, Bishop of Tarbes, made his findings public: he authenticated the apparitions and the message of Lourdes without reservation.

[1] Bernadette received her First Communion on June 3, 1858.
[2] The Hospice served as both a hospital and a school.

During these years, Bernadette struggled continually with illness, but she offered up her physical and emotional suffering "for sinners", as the Holy Virgin had asked her to do, and for the intentions of others. Bernadette suffered from asthma on a regular basis; in addition, at the end of March 1862, she caught pneumonia, and on April 28, 1862, she received last rites for the first time. Astonishingly, Bernadette recovered from the pneumonia almost immediately, but she continued to suffer from asthma for the rest of her life.

Bernadette knew she wanted to consecrate herself to religious life, but she did not know to which congregation she should belong. To four young women who visited her before leaving to become postulants at the Convent of Saint-Gildard, she made this cryptic statement: "I am supposed to become a nun, but I do not know with which order. The Holy Virgin did not tell me. I am waiting."[3] *In addition, in spite of the fact that many congregations were encouraging Bernadette to join them, she had doubts about being accepted into any of them because of her poor health.*

On September 25, 1863, the Bishop of Nevers, Monsignor Forcade, visited Bernadette in Lourdes and asked her about her vocation. She told him that she was giving it great consideration, but she had not yet decided. Unbeknownst to Bernadette, Mother Louise Ferrand, Superior General of the Congregation, was opposed to her joining the Sisters of Nevers. Upon discovering this, the stunned Bishop asked why and reminded her that Bernadette was being sought out by many other congregations. Mother Ferrand responded that Bernadette was constantly sick and would never be anything more than "a regular in the infirmary". She continued: "she does not know how to do anything", so in essence, she would

---

[3] "Je dois être religieuse. Je ne sais pas de quel Ordre. La Sainte Vierge ne me l'a pas dit. J'attends." *Je dois* can be translated as "I am supposed to", "I must", or in some cases, "I should".

not be useful. Bishop Forcade replied: "She can always peel carrots as I have seen her do in Lourdes." In view of the fact that the Holy Virgin did not consider Bernadette's poor health and lack of education to be an impediment, one cannot help but be surprised at Mother Ferrand's opposition. Three months later, Mother Ferrand was replaced by Mother Joséphine Imbert. Finally, in early 1866, Bernadette was accepted as a postulant in the Congregation of the Sisters of Charity and Christian Instruction, or the Sisters of Nevers.

"Love humility."

(From Father C. Alix to Bernadette, June 21, 1863)

This letter from Father Alix to Bernadette is one of the few letters included in the collection that was written to her rather than by her. Father Alix' spiritual advice succinctly reflects Bernadette's spiritual life. In fact, this letter was so important to Bernadette that she took the trouble to recopy it around 1873–1874, a full ten years after she received it. "Love humility, simplicity and suffering" and live a holy life without calling attention to yourself: Bernadette struggled to follow Father Alix' advice for the rest of her life. We meet her as she truly was in these few words.

Father Alix held a doctorate from the Sorbonne and he was known as an outstanding speaker. On April 4, 1865, he gave the inaugural speech at the Grotto before twenty thousand pilgrims when the Statue of the Immaculate Conception was blessed.

My Dear Sister in Our Lord Jesus Christ,

In parting, I would like to leave you with a few thoughts on holiness that I hope will help in your sanctification. Meditate on them from time to time.

1. Love humility. Love believing that you are nothing before God, who alone will fill your heart. Flee from praise. The gospels tell us that God alone is good.

2. Love simplicity. Do not try to rise above your station. Remain in the same station where the Most Holy Virgin found you.

3. Love suffering. Jesus suffered so much for us and his Mother shared so much in his sufferings. Our suffering united to the Passion of Jesus Christ is life giving. It is the sweetest thing on earth.

4. Give the appearance of living on earth as long as it pleases God to leave you here, but in reality, live in Heaven in your thoughts, your emotions and your desires.

I hope you have that wound of divine love in your heart that will never heal in this life.

Dear Sister, do these things and you will have true life.

And finally, my dear Sister in Jesus Christ, I ask you not to forget my poor soul that God himself has sent to you, just as he has sent yours to me. I have the firm belief that by your prayers you are working for my sanctification. You may be assured that I will not allow a single day to pass without presenting you to God at the holy altar during the holy Sacrifice of the Mass.

And finally, my dear Sister, I bless you in the name of the Father, the Son and the Holy Spirit. *Amen.*

One final word: along with humility, obedience.

C. Alix, priest.

Prayer from the Miraculous Medal

(July 30, 1863)

Bernadette copied down the following prayer in a brief note to an unidentified recipient. The prayer comes from the Miraculous Medal. It encircles a figure of the Holy Virgin and it is also inscribed over the altar at the Chapel of the Miraculous Medal in Paris, rue du Bac. In 1830, the Blessed Virgin had appeared to Catherine Labouré, a simple and uneducated nun, asking her to have the medal struck. It took many years for Saint Catherine to accomplish her mission, but when the medal was finally distributed, there were many miraculous healings attributed to it almost immediately. Saint Catherine was aware of the apparitions at Massabielle. Although we have every reason to believe she was gratified that the Virgin appeared in Lourdes, she was saddened by how long it took her superiors to believe her and to follow the directives she had received from the Queen of Heaven. Saint Catherine was convinced that the Blessed Virgin would have done much more through the apparitions in Paris had there not been so many obstacles. She also suspected that it was the opposition to the Holy Virgin's mission in Paris that prompted her to appear in Lourdes.

"O Mary, conceived without sin, pray for us who have recourse to you."

Bernadette Soubirous

Lourdes, 30 July 1863

"Pray that I will not misuse the great favor I have received from Heaven."

(To Don Antonio Moralès, December 3, 1862)

Don Antonio Moralès, an ardent dévoté of Lourdes, was taking up a collection in the province of Malaga to build the sanctuaries. Through these efforts, he maintained a correspondence with the Bishop of Tarbes. Bernadette responded politely, but in a non-committal fashion, to his inappropriate curiosity. The letter is significant because it demonstrates how humble Bernadette was even from the beginning of her apostolic life. In spite of praise and attention from throngs of admirers, she preferred to remain hidden and small so the focus would always remain on the heavenly message, never on her.

December 3, 1862

Monsieur,

I have indeed received your most worthy letter, but I was unable to respond before now. I needed someone's help to answer you, for I am a poor, ignorant girl.

Monsieur, I bless the Lord for your great love and tender devotion for our good Mother, the Most Holy Virgin Mary Immaculate.

Please pray for her intercession for me. May her divine Son grant me the grace to faithfully fulfill all God's plans for me. Monsieur, I am weak. I truly need the help of good souls to pray that I will not misuse the great favor I have received from Heaven, and this in spite of my unworthiness.

Monsieur, I beseech you, your family and your friends to pray for me. In appreciation of your kindness, I promise never to forget you before God and the Immaculate Virgin.

The Rosary is my favorite prayer. I am too ignorant to compose one of my own. Of the various objects you asked of me, I regret that I can only send you a medal of the blessed Grotto. This is all I have right now, but perhaps another time I will be more fortunate. In this hope, Monsieur, accept the homage of my profound respect in the Sacred Hearts of Jesus and Immaculate Mary.

Your very humble servant,

Bernadette Soubirous

"My poor heart would have so many things to tell you."

(To Mother Ursula Fardes, May 2, 1864)

In this touching, yet measured letter, Bernadette hinted at a spiritual suffering that "her poor heart" longed to share with Mother Ursula Fardes. Mother Fardes was the Superior of the Sisters of Lourdes at the time of the apparitions. This letter is all the more striking when contrasted with the matter-of-fact way the twenty-year-old visionary informed Mother Fardes that she was not expected to live much longer. The source of her spiritual suffering remains a mystery, but it is reasonable to surmise that it was closely tied to the messages she received from the Holy Virgin: "Penance! Pray for poor sinners." Bernadette suffered from this same cross until her death in 1879.

While living at the hospice in Lourdes, Bernadette was entrusted to the care of Sister Victorine Poux, and the two shared a deep friendship. In addition, Bernadette helped Sister Aurélie Gouteyron in her work in the infirmary, and she became very attached to Sister Aurélie. This was the first time Bernadette worked in an infirmary, but it was not the last. She spent years in the infirmary at Saint-Gildard, both as a nurse and a patient.

The ladies to whom Bernadette referred are the de Lacour sisters, who lived in Chasselay, near Lyon. The statue is the one that now stands in the niche at the Grotto where the Blessed Virgin appeared to Bernadette. Bernadette's new brother is Jean Soubirous, born on February 4, 1864.

My Dear Mother,

I am taking advantage of this opportunity to talk to you, and I assure you, dear Mother, it does me so much good. It would be an even greater pleasure if God granted me the grace to see you even for a moment. My poor heart would have so many things to tell you. I do not dare say more in writing than to ask you to please pray for me, for I truly need it. I am still ill, but I have been feeling a little better for the last few days. They think I have pneumonia. In any case, may God's will be done. I am resigned to the likelihood of dying, so pray for a good death for me. I think of you often. Every day I pray that God and the Holy Virgin will grant you everything you ask of them, and I pray for your intentions in a special way when I am blessed with the joy of going to the Grotto.

Sister Victorine sends her regards. She loves you so much. We often talk about you and Sister Aurélie, whom the

Mother General took from us last week. They did not request her specifically; they only asked us to send a Sister to Oloron. Our dear Mother chose her especially as a kind of retreat for her. I hope the Holy Virgin will send her back to us. Mother wrote to Nevers about it.

Father Peyramale took a trip with the ladies who offered the statue of the Holy Virgin. I think he is going to Rome.

The whole family sends their regards, especially my sister. By the way, I have a new little brother.

I shall stop my scribbling now, but I am sending you a thousand kisses, along with all my heart. I am also sending you a picture so you will pray for me, but I suspect that you already do.

Dear Mother, please know how grateful and devoted I am to you.

Your obedient servant,

Bernadette Soubirous

Lourdes, May 2, 1864

"I thought I was going home to God."

(To the de Lacour sisters, May 1864)

The unmarried and very devout de Lacour sisters had offered to have a statue made for the Grotto because of their profound devotion to Our Lady of Lourdes. Fabisch, who was considered to be the best sculptor at the time, was commissioned to sculpt the Virgin of the Apparitions. The statue was blessed on April 4, 1864, but Bernadette was too ill to attend. Although Bernadette spent many hours with the sculptor, giving him a meticulous description of the Holy Virgin as she had appeared during the apparitions, she was never satisfied with Fabisch's artistic vision. It depicted a mature woman rather than the tiny young maiden she had described. Bernadette always preferred the small statue of Our Lady of the Waters that still stands in a corner at the far end of the garden at the Convent of Saint-Gildard. She used to say that in some way it resembled the lady of her visions. The de Lacour sisters had great affection for Bernadette and they kept up a regular correspondence with her.

The only version of this letter that still exists is a draft, and it lacks Bernadette's signature. At the time of the apparitions, Bernadette could neither read nor write, and she did not speak French. The Blessed Mother spoke to her in her native patois. The Sisters of Charity and Christian Instruction at the Hospice in Lourdes taught Bernadette to speak, read and write in French. All of her early letters began in draft form; a Sister would correct her spelling, grammar and punctuation, and Bernadette would rewrite the letter correctly. Most of the letters that exist exclusively as drafts lack a signature.

Father Pomian was Bernadette's confessor and the chaplain of the hospice and the prison.

Dear Ladies,

I am taking advantage of a spare moment to thank you for your kindness. I do not know how to express my appreciation for all the gifts you sent me through Father Pomian, especially the pretty book. It makes me happy every time I look at it and I say to myself: there is the book the de Lacour sisters sent. I remember you and Father before God and the Most Holy Virgin so often, especially when I am fortunate enough to go to the Grotto, where I pray for all your intentions.

I am overwhelmed by visitors every day and it wears me out. Recently, I had such a serious attack that I thought I was going home to God. When Father Pomian arrived at the Hospice at nine in the evening I was unconscious. I still feel the effects a little, but last Sunday I was able to go to the Grotto. Be assured that I did not forget you when I was there.

Please excuse me for taking so long to express my appreciation. It was not due to any negligence on my part, I assure you, for I have been thinking of you often. It was only my illness that kept me from writing for so long.

I wish I could express how grateful I am to you and Father Blanc. Please remember me in your holy prayers. As for me, I promise never to forget you in mine, however feeble they may be.

"Let us be in union through prayer for life."

(To Father Charles Bouin, July 9, 1864)

Father Bouin, a priest who wanted to become a hermit at Massabielle, became the privileged recipient of one of the autographed accounts of the apparitions. It was common for pilgrims to request such an account, but it was rare for Bernadette to comply. Father Bouin had a secret hope of establishing a hermitage at Lourdes and Bernadette promised to pray for his intention and to keep his secret in the strictest confidence. This secrecy lends the air of a plot

*to these two letters. As for the picture, many pilgrims gave Berna-
dette photographs of themselves and asked her for one in return.*

*Father Bouin's dream of a hermitage never materialized. In view
of the ever-increasing number of pilgrims, Lourdes might have seemed
an unlikely place for a hermitage; however, most of the activities
were concentrated in a relatively small area. The beautiful moun-
tainous region that lies just beyond the center of the small town
was inviting and led easily to reflection. During the colder months
there were few, if any, pilgrims.*

Dear Father Bouin,

You cannot imagine the sweet joy I felt in receiving your
worthy letter. I was anxious to hear from you. I am so happy
to know you remember me in your holy prayers, especially
at the Holy Sacrifice of the Mass. As for me, I pray for you
also, especially when I am blessed with the joy of going to
the Grotto. Father, if you will agree to it, let us be in union
through prayer for life, for I felt an attachment to you the
first time I met you. I cannot explain it, but it is the good
Lord himself who did it and everything he does is good. I
trust you as much as one person can possibly trust another.

You asked me if I truly understood what you meant when
you said I could be of great help to you. Alas! Miserable
creature that I am, I believe just the opposite, Father, that
it is you who are of great help to the salvation of my soul.
I pray that our good Mother will have compassion for us.
She knows we can do nothing without her help, so she
must take pity on her children.

Your kind prayers have truly done me good. Yes, I am
sure of it, and I hope this good will continue, for at the

moment I need your prayers enormously. I wanted so much to write sooner, but constant visits kept me from doing so. Do not think for a moment that it was through any lack of interest, Father. That was not it at all.

I have been to the Grotto four times this week and I remembered you before our good Mother. I hope you will receive what you desire. How could she refuse you? My entire family joins me in sending our most affectionate regards, especially my sister who asks you to remember her in your prayers. Please pray for my brother, the eldest boy, who is quite lazy about doing his homework. He is not always as obedient to our parents as I would hope. I am going to stop my scribbling and ask you once more to remember me in your holy prayers, Father. You can be quite calm about your letter. No one opened it but me. My parents sent for me and it gave me a good opportunity to visit them.

As for the account of the apparitions, I will send it to you next time, Father. I want nothing more than to do it for you, but it is impossible right now. I have to keep climbing up and down these stairs all day long; in fact, I wrote this letter in several sittings. This is what has me so discouraged about my studies. I scarcely take up my pen when I have to stop again.

Father, I respectfully remain your very humble and very devoted servant,

Bernadette Soubirous

Lourdes, July 9, 1864.

P.S.—Father, Madame Forel was kind enough to show me your picture to see if I thought it was a good likeness. It looks just like you, but I was jealous and almost did not give it back to her.

"Please pray that God will either take me home or allow me to become one of his brides very soon."

(To Father Charles Bouin, August 22, 1864)

Dear Father,

Please forgive me for taking so long to write you. Be assured that it was not from of any lack of interest. Oh no! for I have been thinking about it every moment. Actually, I would have preferred not to think about it so much, especially since I could not do anything about it. In fact, I have not even been able to continue my studies for quite some time. All I do is receive pilgrims from morning to night. So I am taking advantage of this spare moment to write a few lines.

Oh, Father, how happy I would be to see you in Lourdes, especially if you were to live here. I am going to pray to God and the Holy Virgin to let you know if you should become a hermit here. How I wish I could do the same, for I am weary of seeing so many people. Please pray for me that God will either take me home or allow me to become one of his brides very soon, for that is my dearest desire, in spite of my unworthiness. I do not know how to thank you for all your kindness, especially for remembering me and my family every day at the Holy Sacrifice of the Mass. Father, I am so very grateful to you. For my part, I do not forget you in my feeble prayers either.

I did not mention your letters to Madame Forel; it was she who asked me if I had received a letter from you. I said yes, thinking that perhaps you had mentioned it in your letter to her, for she told me she knew about it and that she had received one also. Other than that, I have not said anything about the letters, not a single word.

You asked me the names of the members of my family. Starting with my father, there is: François, Louise, Marie, Jean-Marie, Augustin, Pierre and Jean. I am not naming the eighth; I think that you have not forgotten her.

Father, it was such a nice surprise to find a picture of you when I opened your worthy letter. I was overcome with joy and I have looked at it many times. Alas! I have to be content to look at it. How can I express my gratitude to you for your kindness? I am still praying for the person you recommended to me. I would be grateful if you would ask her to be so kind as to offer up a small part of her suffering to the Lord in my behalf.

A certain person asked me to implore you to take up a collection for a family in dire need, according to what this other person told me. She insists that I do not mention her name, but I know you know her because you have spoken to me about her several times, and according to what she says you have known her a long time. She says that if you are willing to do this and if you are able to collect something, you should send it to Madame Forel. You may well know whom I mean, but if you do please do not let on because she was so insistent about it.

Everyone in my family sends their regards and joins me in asking you to remember us in your holy prayers.

I will stop my scribbling and wish you perfect health, Father. With the respectful wishes of your most devoted servant,

Bernadette Soubirous

Lourdes, August 22, 1864

"As for the lock of hair, I am expressly forbidden to send it."

(To Madame Douville de Saint-Alire, February 24, 1865)

Madame Douville de Saint-Alire made the trip from Picardy to Lourdes many times before Bernadette entered the Convent of Saint-Gildard in Nevers. Her son even had the good fortune to be present when one of the first healings occurred. Pilgrims flocked to Bernadette, asking her to touch their medals and Rosaries and sign their holy cards with the famous "p.p. Bernadette"[4] (pray for Bernadette). Unfortunately, many pilgrims wanted more and some even went so far as to try to cut off part of her veil if she took part in a procession. In this letter, Madame Saint-Alire requested a lock of her hair. Father Peyramale had expressly forbidden Bernadette to comply with this kind of request, thus she was alleviated of the burden of having to consider such an indelicate entreaty.

J. M. J.

Madame,

I do not know how to thank you for your kindness in sending the photographs. I cannot tell you how happy I was to see the picture of Father Hermann. Your inspiration was a good one, for I had wanted a picture of him. Madame, allow me to express my sincere appreciation. I will pray for your intentions for the people who are dear to you exactly

---

[4] "*Priez pour Bernadette.*"

as you requested, and believe me, Madame, I shall not forget you either. Each time I see the picture of Father Hermann, I shall think of the person who gave it to me.

As for the lock of hair, I am expressly forbidden to send it. If your request were for something that I could offer without disobeying, I would be delighted.

Madame, please be so good as to pray for poor Bernadette who recommends herself especially to your holy prayers. Even though my own are feeble, please believe that you will often be remembered in them.

My dear Mother asks me to remember her to you and she sends her respects.

Respectfully,
Your most devoted and grateful servant,

Bernadette Soubirous

Lourdes, February 24, 1865

"My dearest desire is to be part of the family of the Sisters of Nevers."

(To Mother Augustine Ceyrac, December 4, 1865)

Although Bernadette often gave updates on her health in her letters, she rarely expressed how seriously ill she was or how much she was suffering. This letter is unusual in the detailed description of her illness, yet Bernadette did not indulge in self-pity. Her wish to improve was intimately linked to her desire to join the Sisters of Nevers, for she could not enter the convent until she was well.

My Dear Mother,

Please pardon my delay in thanking you for your kindness. I would have answered your affectionate letter sooner, but I was waiting to see if the pills you sent were of some help. I took them exactly as you suggested and they did help a great deal. My sleep was less restless, my appetite was better and this eternal, exhausting cough seemed to have disappeared. I was happy to see my health improve a little; unfortunately, I soon had a relapse. About two weeks ago, I caught a chill and since then I have been suffering from my same old cough and congestion. I have been feeling a little better for the last two days though. I so wish my health would improve. My dearest desire is to be part of the family of the Sisters of Nevers. Dear Mother, please remember me in your holy prayers so that soon I will be able to give myself completely to our divine Savior.

Even though my prayers are so very imperfect, I address them to Our Lady of Lourdes every day. I pray first for you, dearest Mother, who take such an interest in me, and then for the entire community of Figeac. I think of you all so often.

My dear Mother asks me to express her regrets that she cannot write you now and she asks you to remember her . . . [*several illegible words on the copy of the document*] . . . Dearest Mother, please accept my most respectful good wishes and know how deeply I appreciate you.

Bernadette Soubirous

P.S. If those pills are good for asthma, would you send a box for a gentleman who suffers from it and tell me how much they cost?

"I especially love to remember my friends at the feet of our good Mother" at the Grotto.

(To Monsieur Duvroux, the end of 1865 or beginning of 1866)

Monsieur and Madame Duvroux were family friends who lived close enough to Lourdes to stay in touch, but far enough that the "long trip" would have been difficult for Bernadette because of her poor health. The ceremony to which the Duvroux invited Bernadette was probably the blessing of a religious site or statue.

Work on the altar at the Grotto and the Crypt was behind schedule and the dates for the inauguration had been delayed twice.[5] Bernadette mentioned the new date of February 2, 1866, but the inauguration did not take place until the Monday after Pentecost, May 21, 1866. The altars were consecrated on Friday, May 19, 1866.

Monsieur,

How I long to attend the ceremony, but I would not dare to undertake such a long trip. In the first place, the

[5] July 1865 and then December 8, 1865.

cold is extremely bad for my health, but I suspect it would be useless to ask permission anyway. If it is all right with you, during vacation would be better and we could spend more time together then. Let us all make this small sacrifice. As for me, I am anxious to see you. Sometimes I say to myself: "How happy I would be if Madame Duvroux and her most devout husband could come!" Rarely does a day go by that I do not think of you both, I assure you, especially when I am blessed with the joy of going to the Grotto. I especially love to remember my friends there at the feet of our good Mother.

Monsieur, how can I ever thank you for the kindness you have shown us? I am truly overwhelmed when I think of all you have done for my family and me. My parents join me in wishing you a good and Happy New Year. I always pray to Heaven that you will be richly blessed.

Marie asks me to send her regards. My dear Mother and all the Sisters ask me to remember them to you and they offer their best wishes for your good health.

I shall close, Monsieur, by asking you and your wife to remember me in your holy prayers.

Accept my best wishes and allow me the honor of being your grateful and affectionate,

Bernadette Soubirous

Holy Mass will not be celebrated at the Grotto until the Purification. I will try to find out exactly when that will be and I will let you know.

I hope you will be here that day.

"We hardly had time to baptize her when she flew
to Heaven."

(To Madame Duvroux, spring 1866)

*The ninth child of the Soubirous family was a tiny girl who did
not survive and did not even show up on the Lourdes civil register.*

Madame,

Please excuse me for taking so long to write. You might
easily have thought it was negligence on my part, but that
was not it at all. My mother has been ill for quite some
time. And as you know, Marie was supposed to be a
godmother, but our good Lord arranged otherwise. We had
a little girl, but we did not have long to enjoy her. The
good Lord did not create her for this world. We hardly had
time to baptize her when she flew to Heaven, poor little
angel! As you can imagine, it was a hard blow for my poor
mother, but she is doing a little better now. She talks about
you both often, especially since my sister came back from
her visit with you. She says she is bored in Lourdes now,
and then she says that she cried when she was there, but
she laughed a lot too. If we had not sent for her she would
not have come back until you sent her packing. Can you
believe that naughty little child? She asks me to send you
and your husband all her affection.

Madame, please know how enormously grateful we are
to you and your husband for all your kindness.

Please send our best wishes to the young man who came with you and tell him we look forward to seeing him the next time you are in Lourdes. You cannot imagine how anxious we are to be able to thank you in person.

Madame, please remember me in your holy prayers. I need them more than you know if I am to be able to accept suffering patiently, if this be God's will. As for me, I do not forget you. I think of you both often, especially when I am at the Blessed Grotto.

I'll stop my scribbling now and send you my great affection.

Respectfully,
Your most devoted and grateful,

B. S.

"Tell them that Bernadette has not forgotten them."

(To an unnamed lady, April 18, 1866)

Bernadette often used to say: "I will not forget anyone." When she promised to pray for someone, they could be assured that she would keep that promise, even though she thought that her prayers were "very weak." Like the "Little Flower," Saint Thérèse of Lisieux, Bernadette had total confidence that her vocation of praying for others would continue when she was in Heaven.

J. M. J.

Madame,

Although my prayers are very weak and so unworthy to be granted, nevertheless, I will beg Our Lady of Lourdes with such insistence that she will allow herself to be moved and she will obtain the healing of the young lady for whom you are praying so fervently. Let us pray with confidence: our good Mother will not refuse us this grace.

I remember the lady who came to see me perfectly. She was with two young ladies and they asked me to pray for them. Madame, be good enough to tell them that Bernadette has not forgotten them and that they have a great share in all my intentions. In return, I ask them to have the kindness to remember me a little at the feet of our tender Mother.

The entire community is going to begin a novena for all of your intentions. Let us pray with confidence and let us be assured in advance that our perseverance will obtain the graces that we are requesting with such ardor.

My dear Mother asks me to offer her respects to you and the other ladies. She has not forgotten the conversations that she had with you and she asks for your prayers. She asks if you will say a little prayer to Saint Joseph for our chapel that is under construction and that has remained unfinished for so long due to a lack of funds. The graces we have already received from this great protector are so numerous that we have good reason to hope he will not ignore our supplications.

Madame, please be united with us and rest assured that you have not been forgotten in Lourdes.

Madame, accept the most respectful regards from your very humble servant,

Bernadette Soubirous

Lourdes, 18 April 1866.

"I feel more anxious than ever to leave the world"

(To Mother Augustine Ceyrac, April 28, 1866)

It had been decided that Bernadette would go to Nevers, but the date was uncertain, for her health was not good. Then too, the Bishop of Tarbes wanted to keep her in Lourdes through the summer to attract and welcome pilgrims.

In her own letter to Mother Ceyrac,[6] Mother Alexandrine Roques expressed her desire for Bernadette to leave for Nevers as soon as possible. She was concerned that all the attention Bernadette was receiving might negatively affect her natural sense of humility. In addition, Bernadette was being solicited by "all the other orders" to join their congregations, and this in the presence of the Sisters of Nevers who had sheltered and educated Bernadette from the beginning. Mother Roques was afraid that their "covetousness" might lead Bernadette to join another congregation. She wrote that the Sisters of Nevers had never done anything to pressure Bernadette to join them; nevertheless, it was clear that people from all walks of life understood that being close to Bernadette was advantageous.

---

[6] Mother Alexandrine Roques sent both her own letter dated May 1, 1866, and Bernadette's letter to Mother Ceyrac.

In the following letter, Bernadette expressed her deep appreciation to Mother Ceyrac and she referred to her intention of joining the Sisters of Nevers. In fact, in a letter dated May 26, 1866, she was already referring to the Sisters of Nevers as "our community".

J.M.J.
Lourdes, April 28, 1866

Dearest Mother,

It was so kind of you to send the pills. Thank you so much. I have not had another crisis since I took the ones you sent the first time. God has truly blessed me this winter. I think he sent you to Lourdes to heal me. Even though my health has improved, I am still taking the new pills you sent so generously and I am enormously grateful to you.

Thank you for your holy prayers to the Lord for me. I think they have already been answered, for I feel more anxious than ever to leave the world. And now that I have decided, I want to leave as soon as possible. Oh! Dear Mother, how I long for the joyful day when I will enter the Novitiate, for it must truly be a kind of Heaven on earth. Dear Mother, please redouble your holy prayers for my intention. For my part, I promise that I pray for you often. Every time I go to the Grotto, I pray for you and for all your dear Sisters. I unite my plea with yours to obtain the grace that you are seeking.

I am sending you a Rosary that touched the Holy Sepulcher of Our Lord Jesus Christ. It was blessed by Our Holy Father the Pope, and I have prayed with it. I beg you to pray it once for me. It has no monetary value, but it is precious nonetheless.

If I could have sent you one in silver by mail, I would have. I thought you would prefer this one anyway though.

In closing, I thank you once again for your many kindnesses. I will never forget all that you have done for me.

> Respectfully,
> Your very humble servant,
>
> Bernadette Soubirous

"The good Lord will never be outdone in generosity."

(To Monsieur Mouret, father of Léontine Mouret, May 26, 1866)

Léontine Mouret, Bernadette's good friend, aspired to enter the novitiate of the Sisters of Charity and Christian Instruction in Nevers. She was only seventeen years old and her father wanted her to wait until she was older. Bernadette encouraged Monsieur Mouret to allow Léontine to leave with her sooner. Léontine indeed accompanied Bernadette to Nevers, where she was known in religion as Sister Alexandrine. Léontine died at the young age of twenty-three, after only five years of religious life.

J. M. J.   Lourdes, May 26, 1866

Monsieur,

Do not be surprised at receiving a letter from me. Knowing your daughter's ardent desire to join our community, I am writing to beg you to give your consent. This has been her heart's desire for so long and it will bring her such joy. I understand what a great sacrifice it is for a father and mother to see themselves separated from a cherished daughter, but please be generous to the good Lord, who will never be outdone in generosity. Since he asks this of you, be charitable to him and he will repay you. I assure you that he will compensate you for all the little sacrifices you make, and one day, you will be delighted to have given him your child. You can do no better than to put her in the Lord's hands.

How much greater the sacrifice would be to entrust her to a man whom you might not know and who might make her unhappy, while refusing her to the King of Heaven and earth. No, Monsieur, you are much too pious to do such a thing. On the contrary, I think you should thank the Lord, for he is granting you and your daughter a great grace. She understands that.

So I beg of you to decide as soon as possible, for if you wish to let her leave with me, it will be very soon. The trip will be much more pleasant if we make it together, and when we arrive at Nevers, we will get used to everything more quickly.

Léontine does not want to leave without having seen Bétharram, which means that Marie will not return home

until next Wednesday. As for Léontine, we will keep her
with us until you come back and give your consent.

Respectfully,
Your very humble servant,
Bernadette Soubirous

"Pray that God will make me a holy Religious."

(To Mother X, June 15, 1866)

*Although there is some controversy about the person to whom this
letter was addressed, it was very likely written to Mother Ursule
Fardes, who was Superior at the time of the apparitions and for
the three years that followed. In any case, the tone is simultaneously respectful and affectionate, the style unaffected and spontaneous. Since this letter was only a draft, Bernadette signed it
with her initials.*

My Dear Mother,

Knowing the interest you have shown in me, I am happy
to be able to tell you that I have finally made up my mind
to enter your dear congregation. O, my dear Mother, how
happy I would be if I could see you before leaving. I am
afraid that would be difficult, being as hurried as I am to

arrange my affairs, for I hope to leave at the beginning of next month with Léontine Mouret.

Dearest Mother, please remember me in your holy prayers and ask your dear Sisters to pray for me also that God will make me a holy Religious and that I will respond well to the graces he grants me.

My dear Mother, I do not know how to thank you for all your kindness. I am truly embarrassed every time I think of it. All I can do is pray to the Father of mercy to repay you a hundredfold all that you have done for me.

I think of you very often, dear Mother. I love to remember the day when we were at the woodshed and you talked to me about my vocation. How many times I remember that little conversation. I can still see you sitting on one step and me on the other. I look at those steps every time I pass by, and I remember you every time I go to the Blessed Grotto. That is where I pray to our good Mother to grant you all the graces you need. I made a special intention for you the day when I was blessed to attend the Holy Sacrifice of the Mass and to receive the Holy Eucharist for the first time at the underground church at the Grotto.

Mesdemoiselles Estrade and Caroline Dauzat send their regards and fond wishes to you.

My dear Mother and all the Sisters asked me to remember them to you.

Dearest Mother, be assured of my affection and respect.

> Your very humble and
> appreciative child,
>
> B. S.

Bernadette was born at the Boly Mill on January 7, 1844. Her father ran this mill quite successfully for ten years, but with the struggling local economy and many other mills springing up and following an accident in which he lost his left eye, the family was reduced to poverty.

The Soubirous family (of six) was allowed to live in the abandoned village prison, a one-room cell, for the more than two-year period of destitution. The room measured twelve by fifteen feet.

This striking pose of Bernadette at age 22, was taken
by photographer Philippe Viron on July 2, 1866 —
two days before her departure from Lourdes. Today,
the Viron family continues to operate a photography
studio in Lourdes. A rare, life-size photograph of
Bernadette in this pose was developed by the Viron
family and today graces one of the museum walls at the
Shrine of St. Bernadette in Albuquerque, New Mexico.

Father Marie-Dominique Peyramale was the parish priest to whom Bernadette reported the apparitions. At first, Father was quite impatient and stern with the fourteen year-old visionary. In the end, however, Father Peyramale was her strongest supporter and friend. He died on the feast of Our Lady's Birthday, September 8, 1876, preceding Bernadette into Eternity. He served his parishioners at Lourdes for twenty-two years.

The grotto was Bernadette's "Heaven on earth". Here, she is kneeling before a statue of Our Lady that was temporarily placed in the niche until the official sculpture by Joseph Fabisch was installed and dedicated in March of 1864. This photograph was taken by Paul Dufour in October of 1863.

Bernadette was 20 years old during
the time this photograph was taken.
In the early days of photography, models
sat without moving for several minutes
during the taking of photographs. This
is the reason so many of Bernadette's
photographs appear blurred.

In October of 1864, Paul Dufour arranged for
Bernadette be taken to Studio Annet at Tarbes,
12 miles from Lourdes, where she was photographed.
These two photographs were taken during this second
session. Another series of photographs was taken a
year earlier.

The Sisters of Charity and Christian Instruction were founded by Father Jean-Baptiste Delaveyne in Saint-Saulge, France in 1680. During the French Revolution the congregation disbanded. But immediately after, the Sisters rebuilt their religious community. In 1856 this Motherhouse was built in Nevers. During Bernadette's novitiate, 1866, there were 132 novices and 30 postulants attached to this convent. Today, the convent welcomes pilgrims who journey to venerate the incorrupt body of "their saint".

Philippe Viron took this photograph of Bernadette just two days before she left for the Sisters' Motherhouse in Nevers, France, 466 miles from Lourdes. Bernadette is seated in the middle, and although she had not yet been invested in the religious habit of the congregation, the nuns "dressed her up" for this photograph.

The infirmary became Bernadette's home for the better part of her last years on earth. The statue of Our Lady of Lourdes on the mantel is the same image to which Bernadette spoke her last words: "Pray for me, a poor sinner!" The canopy marked with a cross, was Bernadette's bed which she often called her "white chapel". She died in the armchair at 3:00 P.M. on April 16, 1879, at the age of 35.

The bronze and crystal shrine, which was created in the workshop of Armand Caillat Cateland in Lyons, France, was delivered to the Motherhouse on July 18, 1925. The Sisters carefully prepared the saint's body, which was to be placed in the elegant shrine, and it was officially transferred to the Motherhouse chapel on August 3, 1925. The reliquary has been cradling Bernadette's body for public veneration ever since. A continuous procession of pilgrims visit the beautiful Bernadette daily, and they not only pray before her remains, they also take the time to light candles and leave her gifts and messages. The letters ND represent the words *Notre Dame* (Our Lady).

In 1909, the body of Bernadette was exhumed, after being buried in the ground for 30 years, in preparation for the Ecclesiastical Inquiry into her life and miracles. Although Bernadette's habit was damp and her Rosary had rusted, she was found perfectly incorrupt. The Sisters cleansed her body, changed her habit, and returned her to the earth. Ten years later, 1919, a second exhumation was ordered. Again, the saint's body was found incorrupt. She was returned to her grave. Six years later, in 1925, she was exhumed for the third and last time. It was then decided to enshrine her incorrupt body in the Mother-house chapel for public veneration.

Detail of the face and hands of the incorrupt body of
Saint Bernadette Soubirous. 1995 photograph by Dan Paulos.

Three-in-one basilicas were erected on the sight of the 18 apparitions of Our Lady. The first chapel to be built was the crypt. It was completed before Bernadette left Lourdes in 1866. She had the privilege of praying in the crypt, rejoicing that Our Lady's wishes had come true. In 1876 the upper basilica was built on top of the crypt. Scenes of the apparitions are portrayed in the beautiful stained glass windows. This chapel is dedicated to the Immaculate Conception. The church of the Holy Rosary was added in 1889. This majestic chapel is best known for its crown-like dome. The Mysteries of the Rosary are rendered in exquisite mosaic tiles in each of the 15 small chapels encircling this large basilica. On the right flows the River Gave. Bernadette's beloved Grotto is located just behind the basilicas, facing the Gave.

CHAPTER 4

Postulant and Novice at the Convent of Saint-Gildard
1866–1867

At long last, Bernadette arrived in Nevers to begin her postulancy on July 7, 1866. The following day, she stood before the assembled members of the community and publicly shared her story of the apparitions of the Holy Virgin with them for the first and the last time. On the 29th of July, she received her habit and her name in religion, a name very dear to her heart: henceforth, Bernadette was known as Sister Marie-Bernard. She was assigned the job of nurse's aid in the infirmary, but during her first year at Saint-Gildard she spent as much time as a patient there as she did as an aid. Crowds came to the Convent of Saint-Gildard in hopes of seeing the young visionary; however, Mother Imbert refused in all but exceptional cases.

By mid-August, Bernadette fell ill, in effect beginning what she eventually referred to as her "job of being ill". She was confined to the infirmary, where she remained until February. In October 1866, the state of her health was so desperate that she received last rites and was allowed to make her vows in articulo mortis. *The Journal of the Community records: "Sister Marie-Bernard pronounced her vows with angelic zeal. Afterward, she began to improve." That evening, Mother Vauzou, Mistress of Novices, wanted to watch over her, but Bernadette declared: "No, I will not die tonight." Tradition has it that Mother Vauzou responded in frustration: "Why didn't you say so before then?" For the second time, Bernadette's health began to improve after receiving last rites. As Mother Ferrand had feared, Bernadette was indeed "a regular in the infirmary". She required another four months of convalescence. In February she began to take part in community life again as best she could. On October 30, 1867, she had the joy of making her first profession (again) with forty-five other novices. After making her first profession, the Bishop, Monsignor Forcade, asked Mother Imbert what job he should assign to her. Mother Imbert replied: "She is not good at anything." Monsignor Forcade assigned her the "job of praying" and added that she would also serve as a nurse's aid under Sister Marthe Forest, who was in charge of the infirmary.*

"The Grotto is where you will find me in spirit, clinging to the foot of the rock I love so much."

(To the Sisters at the Hospice in Lourdes, July 20, 1866)

This is the earliest surviving letter from Bernadette's first days as a postulant at the Convent of Saint-Gildard. She began her letter by teasing the Sisters at the Hospice in Lourdes, demonstrating the level of comfort and familiarity she had acquired with them. Despite a teary first day, she soon became devoted to life at the convent.

A July 7th entry in the Journal of the Community *expressed the joy the community experienced in receiving this celebrated visionary. "At last our prayers have been answered! Bernadette is in the novitiate! How anxious we have been to have this privileged visionary of the Grotto of Lourdes among us! She is exactly as she is reputed to be: humble, simple, modest, smiling and sweetly happy in spite of her long illnesses."*

Bernadette recounted the events of Massabielle to her new Community on Sunday, July 8, and the Sisters were thenceforth strictly forbidden to ask her about it. The Journal recorded: " 'My secret is for me.' The Holy Virgin told her things she is not to reveal to anyone. Happy creature who at the age of fourteen was blessed with these mysterious conversations with the Queen of Angels."

Crowds came to the convent asking to see her, but for the most part, the superiors refused. To Bernadette's dismay and disappointment, they relented for certain prelates and distinguished benefactors; however, they needed to search all over the convent to find her. "They promised me!" she would respond when discovered; nevertheless, she obeyed and was always polite in the presence of the guests.

In this first letter from Saint-Gildard, Bernadette expressed a sentiment that she would often repeat: "The Grotto is where you will find me in spirit, clinging to the foot of the rock I love so much."

My Very Dear Sisters,

You must be anxious to hear from me. I can almost hear you calling me indifferent! I do not mind. I am so used to your meanness now that my poor heart is immune to it.

Let me tell you all about the trip. We arrived in Bordeaux Wednesday evening at six o'clock, and we stayed there until Friday at one o'clock. I assure you that we took advantage of the time to get out and see things, and in a carriage, if you please. We were taken to visit all the houses. They certainly do not resemble the one in Lourdes,[1] especially

[1] Bernadette was probably referring to the Hospice in Lourdes where she had lived with the Sisters of Nevers.

the *Institution impériale.*[2] It is more like a palace than a religious house! We went to see the Des Carmes church and from there we drove to the Garonne River to see the ships. Next, we went to the *Jardin des Plantes*[3] and we saw something new. You will never guess what! Goldfish: red, black, white, gray. It was so beautiful to see those little things swimming around with a crowd of little children watching them.

We slept in Périgueux on Friday and the next day we set out at seven o'clock in the morning and arrived in Nevers around ten thirty at night.

Léontine and I cried all day long Sunday. The good Sisters encouraged us by saying that it was a sign of a good vocation. Rest assured that the sacrifice would be even more bitter if we had to leave our dear novitiate now. One senses that this is truly God's house, so you cannot help loving it in spite of yourself! I feel his presence everywhere, especially in our dear mistress' instructions; her every word goes straight to my heart. I pray to the Lord constantly to thank him for all the graces that he bestows on me every day. Dear Sisters, please pray for this intention for me, especially when you go to the Grotto. That is where you will find me in spirit, clinging to the foot of the rock that I love so much. I especially ask you to remember me in your holy prayers before our good Mother. As for me, I remember you before the statue of Our Lady of the Waters that is at the end of the garden in a sort of Grotto. That is where I went to pour my heart out my first days here, and since then our dear mistress has allowed us to go there every evening.

[2] The Imperial Convent School was a school for deaf-mutes.
[3] City gardens.

I pray to the Holy Virgin for my dear Sister Victorine and I ask her to take pity on her and dry her tears. My beloved Sister V.,[4] please kiss the two little Lacaze children and Francine and Léonie for me. I send them my best until they come here to see me. Please tell all the students that I am thinking of them, especially my dear friend Léontine Pomian. Ask her to please give my respects to Mademoiselle P.[5] and tell her that, in spite of the distance, I have not forgotten her. Ask her to pray for me sometimes.

My good Sisters, please tell Father Peyramale that I send him my most sincere respects. Ask him to remember me in his holy prayers and to ask the congregation to pray for me too. I would be most grateful if he left my name on the list of members of the parish.

I close, my good Sisters, by sending you a kiss with all my heart. Be assured of my profound respect.

Your very humble and grateful child,

Bernadette Soubirous

"I am more and more aware of my weakness."

(To Monsignor Laurence, Bishop of Tarbes, August 21, 1866)

Although this letter is official and even formulaic at times, it demonstrates Bernadette's response of true joy and humility at receiving

[4] Bernadette means Sister Victorine Poux.
[5] Mademoiselle P. refers to Léontine Pomian, Father Pomian's sister.

her habit and her name in religion: Sister Marie-Bernard. Berna-
dette was devoted to Saint Bernard, her patron saint; she copied
long texts related to him in notebooks and on bits of paper. The
experience of becoming "Sister Marie-Bernard" marked a turning
point for Bernadette as she realized more than ever that the great
grace she received from the Queen of Heaven brought with it enor-
mous responsibilities.

Monsignor,

As happy and welcome as I feel in this pious and holy
sanctuary where the good Lord has led me and where I
enjoy the sweetest peace and the purest joy, I have not forgotten the profound respect and great appreciation I owe
your Lord Bishop. So I take the liberty of kneeling at your
feet to beg your fatherly blessing. As a little lamb in your
flock, I need your help and grace to respond to the many
blessings I have received from the Lord.

I am more and more aware of my weakness, especially
since I had the great joy of being clothed in the holy habit
of a Religious and receiving the names Marie-Bernard, names
that are so beautiful and so dear to my heart. Although this
has given me joy, it also imposes great responsibilities that I
must fulfill.

Monsignor, please accept the homage of my profound
respect. In Our Lord, I have the honor of being your Lord
Bishop's very humble and submissive daughter,

Sister Marie-Bernard Soubirous

Nevers, August 21, 1866

"I do not think the good Lord has finished testing
me yet."

(To Mother Augustine Ceyrac, September 3, 1866)

My Dear Mother,

I am happy to be able to write and thank you for sending the pills. I really do not know how to express my great
appreciation for all your kindness to me. I do not think the
good Lord has finished testing me yet, for since arriving in
Nevers, I have been suffering from stomach aches and head-
aches, but that does not keep me from being contented and
very happy here in the Novitiate where everyone spoils me.

My dear Mother, I am counting on your great sense of
charity and that of your dear Sisters to thank the Lord for
the graces he continues to bestow on me. I promise to do
the same for you and your house.

Give my respects to your sister. I need her prayers. Please
ask her to pray for me in a very special way so that I may
become a devout novice.

Dearest Mother, be assured of my profound respect.

Your very humble and grateful servant,

Sister Marie-Bernard Soubirous

"I offered this painful sacrifice to Our Lord and his Holy Mother."

(To Father Pomian, January 2, 1867)

Louise Soubirous, Bernadette's mother, died at the relatively young age of 41 on December 8, 1866, the feast of the Immaculate Conception. Her death occurred while Vespers of the Immaculate Conception was being sung at the Crypt of the Basilica for the first time, which must have been a source of consolation for Bernadette.

Sister Victorine Poux had visited Madame Soubirous on her way to Vespers and she had promised to write to Bernadette for her. When she returned to the house after Vespers to write the letter, she discovered that Madame Soubirous had died during her absence. Bernadette did not learn about the death until two days later. The letter to which Bernadette referred was written by the Mother Superior of the Hospice in Lourdes.

Dear Father,

I would never have believed that such a painful blow would come to me so soon. I cannot express the pain I felt when I heard that my mother had died so suddenly. I found out that she had died before I even knew she was ill. I understand that they kept her illness a secret to keep me from worrying, but alas, the blow was no less cruel. When I read my dear mother's letter, I had no illusions; my first thought was that my mother was no longer in this world. I offered this painful sacrifice to Our Lord and his Holy Mother and

I took refuge at the foot of their altar to pray for the repose of her soul and to ask them to be with my family. I also asked Our Lord to grant me the grace to be able to carry the cross that he has given me with courage.

Father, I would be very grateful if you prayed for the repose of her soul and for my family.

I often ask Our Lord to keep you in good health and to bestow more and more of his plentiful blessings on you so you will be able to work for a long time to come to make him loved. These are my wishes for you for the New Year.

> Father, accept the respectful affection of your very humble and grateful servant,
>
> Sister Marie-Bernard Soubirous

"I am still a regular in the infirmary."

(To Mother Ursule Fardes, August 16, 1867)

In this letter to Mother Fardes, the Superior of the Hospice in Lourdes, Bernadette alluded to the now famous conversation between Monsignor Théodore-Augustin Forcade, Bishop of Nevers and Mother Louise Ferrand, the former Superior General of the Congregation, when Mother Ferrand had expressed her opposition to Bernadette entering the Novitiate of the Sisters of Nevers.

My Dearest Mother Ursule,

I am happy to spend a few minutes with you. Allow me to express my sincere appreciation to you once more for all your kindness. What can I tell you about myself? I am still a regular in the infirmary.

This time the good Lord has kept me on the cross longer. I have been ill since November. Say a little prayer for me; I certainly need it. One needs patience when it is so long, so ask him to give me a lot of it.

My beloved Mother, I shall close with a kiss. Rest assured that I think of you often.

Sister Marie-Bernard Soubirous

"I felt such joy the day I made my religious profession."

(To Father Peyramale, February 25, 1868)

After receiving last rites for the first time, Bernadette was allowed to make her first profession in articulo mortis *on October 25, 1866. Nevertheless, Canon Law required that a Sister who makes her vows under these circumstances and then regains her health must repeat the process and undergo the usual canonical examination. Bernadette was happy to be able to renew her vows with her companions on October 30, 1867, and she wrote to Father Peyramale about this joy-filled day.*

Gratitude was a cornerstone of Bernadette's spiritual life, but she often felt inadequate in her attempts to thank God. In this letter, she asked Father Peyramale to pray for her, saying she "needs help to thank" Jesus and the Holy Virgin for the many graces they have granted her. She also asked him to ask Our Lord to bless her "with the virtue of humility and a genuine spirit of sacrifice".

Dear Father Peyramale,

Please forgive me for waiting so long to share my happiness. I felt such joy the day I made my Religious profession. I would have repaid the debt gratitude demands earlier if the good Lord had not kept me in bed with several severe illnesses.

Father Peyramale, allow me to thank you for the holy prayers you offered to Heaven for me that day. Please keep praying for me for help to thank Our Lord and his Most Holy Mother for all the graces they have bestowed on me.

Please be good enough, Father, to send my respects to Father Pomian and the Associate Pastors. I thank them for the holy prayers they offered for me.

Recently, I saw a young lady who met you in Rome. She spoke a great deal about you and your trip. I was delighted to discover that you were fortunate enough to see our Holy Father and talk with him. Father, I hope I was included a little in the blessing you surely asked of His Holiness for the flock entrusted to your care.

Father, please remember me in your prayers, especially during the Holy Sacrifice of the Mass. Please ask Our Lord to bless me with the virtue of humility and a genuine spirit of sacrifice.

Please ask the Congregation to pray for me too, Father. I would be very grateful to all the young ladies if they would

pray to Our Lord and his Most Holy Mother for me, especially when they go to my dear Grotto; I need help to thank
them for the many graces they have granted me. I will try
to reciprocate with my own prayers to Our Lord in his
Holy Tabernacle, however weak mine may be.

Father, accept the homage of my profound respect.

> Your very humble and grateful servant,
> Sister Marie-Bernard Soubirous

Nevers, February 25, 1868

CHAPTER 5

Sister Marie-Bernard
1867–1875

During Bernadette's last years in Lourdes, she felt anxious for the day when she would be able to "hide" at the Convent of Saint-Gildard. Much to her disappointment, her celebrity did not come to a sudden halt when she arrived in Nevers. So many bishops visited the convent in the hope of meeting Bernadette that she was finally prompted to quip: "These poor bishops would be better off staying in their own dioceses."

The Bishop of Nevers gave the Bishop of Tarbes permission to send a photographer, who photographed Bernadette in the simple Pyrenean clothing in which she had arrived in Nevers and in her beloved habit. Nineteenth-century photography was not a rapid procedure and Bernadette was required to pose for hours, kneeling much of the time. The photographer wanted her to reproduce the facial expression and physical demeanor she took on during her ecstasy in the presence of the Holy Virgin, an impossible task that must surely have been offensive to her. Profits from the sale of the photographs helped finance the construction of the chapel at the Grotto, the chapel Our Lady requested when she appeared at Massabielle. Upon learning that "Bernadette costs ten sous,"[1] she replied: "I am not worth that much." The convent constantly received requests from people asking Bernadette to pray for their intentions. To guard

---

[1] The pictures cost tourists the modern-day equivalent of a few cents.

her from losing her natural humility, yet grant the requests, the petitions were presented to the entire congregation; Bernadette never suspected that the prayer requests had been addressed directly to her.

These years were filled with many sad events and serious bouts with illness for Bernadette; her reaction was always one of faith. In 1870, the Franco-Prussian War broke out and the convent found itself almost on the front lines; canons were installed on the convent grounds in case of attack, and the Sisters of Nevers received the wounded from nearby battles. The Sisters kept their trunks packed in preparation to evacuate in the event it became necessary. Scarcely did the threat of war pass when, in 1871, civil uprisings in France left scores dead, once again threatening the security of the Sisters of Nevers. Finally, in 1875, the Gave River flooded, causing widespread devastation across the South of France. All the bridges in Toulouse except one were swept away by the raging waters. When news of the flood reached Bernadette in Nevers, naturally, she feared for her loved ones and her beloved Grotto. We can only imagine her sense of relief and gratitude when she learned that the people and places that were so dear to her were safe.

On a more deeply personal level, Bernadette's family suffered one death after another. In 1871, Bernadette's sister Marie lost her first child, and three weeks later her father died unexpectedly. Poor Marie lost one child after another and Bernadette shared her sister's grief intimately. From 1866 to 1873, Bernadette bounced back and forth from working in the infirmary as a nurse's aid to being confined there herself as a patient. On June 3, 1873, she once again fell so ill that she was given last rites for the third time. Her recovery was painstakingly slow, and in October 1873 she was officially relieved of her duties as nurse's aid. In January 1874, having finally recovered, she was given the new employment of sacristan's aid, an assignment intended to be less strenuous than her work in the infirmary; nevertheless, she continued to help in the infirmary when she was able.

On a happier note, Bernadette was overjoyed when her brother Jean-Marie entered the novitiate with the Brothers of Christian Instruction in Ploërmel in 1870. Unfortunately, this joy was short-lived; in 1874, Jean-Marie left religious life permanently without bothering to inform his sister who loved him so dearly and was so concerned for his well-being. She learned this sad news from a third party.

In spite of so many reasons for discouragement and tears, Bernadette saw everything that happened through the eyes of faith. Sister Joseph Vidal testified about her demeanor during those years, saying: "What touched me most was her sweet simplicity and serenity. She was cheerful even to the point of being mischievous during recreation."

"Tell the children to be very good and to say a little 'Hail Mary' for me every day, especially when they go to my dear Grotto."

(To her sister, Marie, April 16, 1868)

This letter to her sister, Marie, is full of affection for the entire family. For Bernadette, affection was intrinsically tied to prayer. Here she asked Saint Joseph to grant all her loved ones "the grace of a holy death", demonstrating to what extent the possibility of death was ever-present to her. She reported that her health was "perfectly good", but the reader should remember that when Bernadette said that she was in "good health" often she simply meant that she was not bedridden. Although she did not try to hide her health problems, she never complained in her letters. Her matter-of-fact and understated style masked the seriousness of her medical condition.

Marie Soubirous married Joseph Sabathé on September 2, 1867. "Bernadette" was Bernadette Nicolau, the daughter of her Aunt Bernarde. The little girl was born in 1863 and was then five years old and a student in the class of Sister Victorine Poux. "Our relatives from Momères" were Thècle (eldest sister of François Soubirous), and Michel Védère, who had five children at the time of this letter. Among them was Bernadette's cousin, Jeanne, her former confidante when they both lived in Lourdes. Jeanne, who was seventeen years older than Bernadette, entered the Cistercian monastery of Blagnac a short time after Bernadette left for Nevers. And finally, "Little Pierre" was Bernadette's youngest brother.

My Beloved Sister,

Let me begin by wishing you, the whole family and all our relatives a joyous Alleluia. Please kiss them all for me and give them my love. Remember me to the children, whom I love. Tell them to be very good and to say a little "Hail Mary" for me every day, especially when they go to my dear Grotto.

I would have written Joseph on his feast day had it not been during Lent. Tell him that I did not forget and that I prayed for him. I especially asked Saint Joseph to make him a devout Christian. I asked him the same for the whole family. Since he is the patron saint of a happy death, I also asked him to grant all of us the grace of a holy death.

Remember me to my uncle and Aunt Lucile. I think of them often. Kiss them for me. Bernadette still attends our dear Sister Victorine's class, doesn't she? Tell her to kiss Sister Victorine for me and to tell her that I am expecting a visit from her this year.

When our relatives from Momères visit you, please give them my best. I would very much like to know if my cousin and François still live at home. Tell them to send me all the news.

My health is perfectly good, so do not worry about me. I am very happy in every possible way.

I close with an affectionate kiss for everyone. Tell Little Pierre that he is charged with giving three big kisses to my father for me.

My very dear family, I send you the respectful heart of your grateful child,

Sister Marie-Bernard Soubirous

"Ask Father Peyramale to pray to God and the Most Holy Virgin for my conversion."

(To Mother Alexandrine Roques, April 6, 1869)

Nevers, April 6, 1869

My Very Dear Mother,

Let me begin by wishing you and your dear daughters a joyous Alleluia.

Mother Marceline told me that you had burned your hand and that Sister Victorine and Sister Orélie have been ill. It goes without saying how sad I was when I found out. My dear Mother, please let me know how all of you are.

Please do not be angry with me for not having written sooner. It was not from lack of desire. I was anxious for the end of Lent so that I could write, but the good Lord decided that I should spend Easter in bed. At first, I was violently ill; it did not last long and I am much better now.

Our Venerable Mother General is still holding her own. Keep praying for her.

Our dear and worthy Mistress asks me to remember her to you.

Dearest Mother, please give my respects to Father Peyramale and Father Pomian. Ask Father Peyramale to pray to God and the Most Holy Virgin for my conversion. My Superiors often tell me that I am willful. It makes me ashamed of myself, but I do not seem to improve.

My dear Mother, please pray for me and ask your daughters to pray for me too. Please remember me to them.

Respectfully,
Your grateful daughter,

Sister Marie-Bernard Soubirous

"How devout you and I should be, my dear brother, in order to thank Our Lord and the Most Holy Virgin."

(To her brother, Jean-Marie, April 21, 1870)

Bernadette was overjoyed to learn that Jean-Marie, her brother, had just entered the novitiate with the Brothers of Christian Instruction (Brothers of Ploërmel). Her advice to him gives us a clear picture of her spiritual life and how it had continued to develop and deepen since her arrival at the convent. In addition, this letter demonstrates Bernadette's vision of consecrated life. Her secret hope

*was that one day her little brother, Pierre, would also "give himself
to the Lord".*

My Dear and Beloved Brother,

I wish I could express the joy my heart felt when I heard
that you had entered the novitiate of the Brothers of Christian Instruction.

How devout you and I should be, my dear brother, in order
to thank Our Lord and the Most Holy Virgin for the signal
grace of having called us to his service, we who are so weak
and so ignorant. Let us apply ourselves to studying the saints
by imitating their virtues of humility, obedience, charity and
self-denial. Let us often remember the words of the divine Master, who tells us: "I have come not to be served, but to serve."
That seems difficult to our nature, but when we love Our Lord,
everything becomes easy. When it is difficult for us, let us
immediately say: "Everything to please you, O My God, and
nothing to please me." Another thought that has done me great
good is: "Always do what costs us the most." This has helped
me overcome several little things that I found loathsome.

My dear brother, thank you for your prayers; pray for
our parents too and especially for little Pierre. I would be
so happy if he gave himself to the good Lord too. In our
prayers, let us not forget sinners and the poor souls in Purgatory, especially our poor relatives.

I was extremely sick this winter; that is what kept me
from writing you sooner. I have been feeling better for the
last few days.

Please give my respects to Father Superior and ask him
and the community to pray for me.

Adieu, my good brother. Remember me next to the Sacred Hearts of Jesus and Mary. That is where I will meet you.

Your devoted sister[2]

"Dear friend, show your gratitude to Our Lord by becoming humble and obedient."

(To her brother, Jean-Marie, December 28, 1870)

Bernadette rejoiced in learning that Jean-Marie had received the habit and his name in religion, Brother Marie-Bernard. Again, she wisely advised him to pray for the virtues of humility and obedience.

Nevers, December 28, 1870

My Dear Brother,

I can not express the joy I felt when I learned that you had been clothed in the livery of Our Lord. What happiness for you.

I thanked the good Master for the signal grace that he has granted you. Every day I pray that you will be clothed in this dear livery until your last day. That is your wish too, I am sure. What increased my joy even more was to see the name "Brother Marie-Bernard" on the bottom of your letter. Dearest brother, I like to think that you are doing every-

---

[2] This letter comes from a copy rather than an original; there is no signature on the copy.

thing in your power to be worthy of the confidence your superiors have shown you in giving you the Holy Habit so soon. Dear friend, show your gratitude to Our Lord by becoming humble and obedient. Let us ask the Most Holy Virgin and the Holy Child Jesus for these two virtues for each other every day. Let us remember that the means of obtaining new graces is to thank Our Lord and the Most Holy Virgin for those that we have already been granted.

I was sick, otherwise I would have written you sooner, but I have been feeling better for the last few days.

I wish you a Happy New Year. I am asking the child Jesus to give you his love and a great spirit of sacrifice as your New Year's gift.

Adieu, my dear brother. Remember me when you are next to the Sacred Hearts of Jesus and Mary. That is where I will meet you.

Your most devoted sister,

Sister Marie-Bernard Soubirous

"On days when we receive the Holy Eucharist, I feel my soul full of strength and confidence when I think that it is no longer I who pray, but Jesus in me."

(To Mother General Joséphine Imbert, May 18, 1870)

Bernadette wrote this letter during the period when she was assigned to the infirmary. Journal entries for the Community and documents relating to the canonization process show her to be exemplary at her work. In this letter, she made light of the abscessed tooth from which she was suffering: "My mouth is lopsided, but I am up and around." Although many have suggested that Mother Imbert was unkind to Bernadette, the tone of this letter is warm, affectionate and even unreserved, suggesting that perhaps such a portrayal is an exaggeration.

It was a difficult time for the Church. Italy was unified, but it threatened the independence of the Pope and the status of the Vatican. On March 26, 1870, Mother Imbert, Bishop Forcade and Sister Eléonore Cassagnes left for Rome to seek pontifical approval to return to the Congregation's original Constitution and teachings of their founder, Dom de Laveyne. The two Sisters did not return until July. Mother Imbert was quite ill during this time, but it was essential that she make the trip. Sister Eléonore's notes of the trip frequently included the name "Sister Marie-Bernard".

My Dear and Venerable Mother,

How I have been longing to write you, but since you left, I have either been busy taking care of our dear patients or I have been sick myself. For the moment, Sister Nathalie is the only patient. She is doing much better and she is beginning to take walks in the hall in the infirmary. As for me, I have been suffering from an abscessed tooth and a swollen cheek. My mouth is lopsided, but I am up and around. I am not losing this opportunity to offer up all the little sufferings and sacrifices God sends me for your intentions so Our Lord and the Most Holy Virgin may bless and answer the desires of your Mother's heart for the greater glory of God and the sanctification of the souls entrusted to your care.

In my prayers, however feeble they may be, I have not forgotten all of those whom you recommended to me before you left. I keep this promise in a special way on days when we receive the Holy Eucharist. I feel my soul full of strength and confidence when I think that it is no longer I who pray, but Jesus in me. I pray especially for the needs of the Council, the Congregation and our Holy Father, the Pope. How happy I would be to receive his blessing!

I was sorry to hear that you are still sick, dear Mother. I hope that we will have the joy of seeing you again soon. It seems like such a long time to us all.

Sister Eléonore sends her regards to you, venerable Mother.

With my profound and affectionate respect.

Your submissive and grateful daughter in Our Lord, Jesus Christ,

Sister Marie-Bernard Soubirous

"I could easily forego seeing the Prussians."

(To her father, November 1870)

France was at war with Prussia and the Sisters of Nevers cared for France's wounded. By the end of November, the Prussians were swiftly approaching toward Nevers and the military authorities prepared to defend the motherhouse from attack. Bernadette remained unafraid and clear headed.

Only an unsigned transcript of this fragment of a letter exists.

They say the enemy is close to Nevers. I could easily forego seeing the Prussians, but I am not afraid of them: God is everywhere, even in the middle of the Prussians. I remember when I was little, after one of Father Peyramale's sermons, I heard some people saying: "Bah! He is only doing his job." It seems to me that the Prussians are only doing their job too ...

"Pray a novena to Our Lady of Lourdes and wash him with water from the Grotto."

(To her sister, Marie, December 25, 1870)

It was a wartime Christmas without Mass at Saint-Gildard. The Prussians had reached the outskirts of Nièvre[3] and all the Sisters who were able were caring for the wounded. By the end of December, the Sisters had packed their bags and were prepared to evacuate if necessary. The beginning of the New Year brought even worse news when they learned that the Holy Father was in danger; however, an armistice was finally signed between France and Prussia on January 28. Despite such harrowing circumstances, Bernadette made only one brief, but faith-filled reference to the war and the danger she was in: "Pray to the Most Holy Virgin to intercede for us with her dear Son to forgive us and to have mercy on us. I have the sweet confidence that God's Justice, which is striking us now, will be softened by his loving Mother." Other than this one reference to the war, she concentrated on her father's

[3] Nièvre is the province in which Nevers is located.

safety, her newborn nephew's medical condition, words of comfort to Laurentine Soubirous, who had not heard from her son, and other family concerns.

My Beloved Sister,

In your letter, you mentioned that father is thinking of coming to see me. I would love to see him too, but please tell him not to come. If by chance something bad happened to him on the way, I would never forgive myself.

Our venerable Mother General promised that she would permit me to see the whole family when the chapel at the Grotto is blessed. I would have been so happy to see father, but the happiness will be even greater to see all of you together. My health is fairly good, so do not worry about me.

My good sister, I can not tell you how sad I was when I found out that my little nephew[4] was born with one foot turned in and that he might be crippled for life. I beg of you, take him to the doctor. Perhaps they can do something for him. Pray a novena to Our Lady of Lourdes and wash him with water from the Grotto.

I am delighted that you made Monsieur Alphonse and Madame Louise Ponson his godparents. Please give them my regards. I often remember them to Our Lord. I have not forgotten their driver's three sons either. I share in his pain, knowing what a position he is in.

---

[4] Bernard-Alphonse-Louis Sabathé was born July 10, 1870.

Please tell Laurentine Soubirous that I pray to the Most Holy Virgin every day to protect her son John. Tell her not to be disappointed if she has not heard from him. They might not have given him permission to write now.

There is only one thing that we can do and that is to pray to the Most Holy Virgin to intercede for us with her dear Son to forgive us and to have mercy on us. I have the sweet confidence that God's Justice, which is striking us now, will be softened by his loving Mother.

My good sister, you reproached me a great deal in your letter. You think that I do not write often enough. I admit it, but what do you want me to say? Since I have nothing new to say, I would just keep repeating the same things. You should be a little more indulgent with me and write three letters to my one. Things would be fine that way. In the meantime, I am anxious for news from you. Please answer as soon as you receive this.

You did not mention Aunt Lucile and her family. Is she angry with me by any chance? I still love her and I think about her often. Give my love to her, as well as to my uncles, aunts and cousins, whom I love dearly.

I close, my dearest family, with an affectionate kiss. My little niece is in charge of giving two big kisses to father for me. If you receive any news from Jean-Marie,[5] please let me know. I am not happy with Pierre.[6] He is too lazy to write me.

Respectfully and gratefully,

Sister Marie-Bernard Soubirous

[5] Bernadette's brother.
[6] Bernadette's youngest brother.

"Let us carry and kiss the cross that our good Jesus has given us."

(To her sister, Marie, March 9, 1871)

Three deaths in the Soubirous family in the span of one month plunged them into deep mourning. Bernadette had not seen her sixty-four-year-old father, François Soubirous, since 1866, and his death made that earthly separation permanent. On learning of her father's death, she said to Sister Madeleine Bounaix: "I have just learned of the death of my father. He died Saturday. Always have a great devotion for the agonizing heart of Jesus, for it is a consolation to know that we have prayed for those we love when we lose them and we cannot be there. That is what I was doing on Saturday, praying for those in the final agony of death, never suspecting that I was praying for my poor father, who at that very moment was entering into eternity."[7]

As if the sudden death of her father were not enough, Marie's daughter, little Bernadette,[8] *and their Aunt Basile's daughter, Marie-Justine, also died. And finally, their Aunt Lucile to whom Bernadette was so close was gravely ill. Little Bernadette died at the age of two and a half on February 12, 1871; François Soubirous died on March 4, 1871; and Aunt Lucile died on March 16, 1871.*

Bernadette responded to all these sad events with faith.

[7] Testimony of Sister Madeleine Bounaix in a letter dated November 22, 1907.

[8] Bernadette's baptismal name was Marie-Bernarde Sabathé. Marie had another daughter in 1874, who was named Bernadette-Irma Sabathé.

My Beloved Sister,

It pleased Our Lord to take what was dearest to us in this world, our dear and beloved father. I am mourning with you; nevertheless, let us remain obedient and resigned to the hand of God that has been striking us such harsh blows recently, even though we are already overwhelmed with grief. Let us carry and kiss the cross that our good Jesus has given us, asking him and the Most Holy Virgin for the strength and the courage to carry it according to their example, without letting ourselves be overcome.

The separation from our dear and beloved father is terribly painful, but our consolation is great since he was blessed to receive the sacraments; let us thank Our Lord for this great grace. Let us pray with faith for the repose of his soul and for our mother's soul. Please have Masses celebrated for them as often as you can.

I am deeply touched by the charity and kindness of our Venerable Mother General, who had a Mass celebrated for our poor father today. The entire community is praying for him and for the family. My good sister, I implore you and Joseph not to give in to grief.

My good sister, I share in the grief your poor mother's heart felt in losing your little Bernadette. Take consolation in knowing that she is a little angel in Heaven who is praying for us now when we need it so much.

It seems that Aunt Lucile is quite ill and perhaps has already died. I am prepared for the worst, so please write and do not hide anything from me. If my aunt is still in this world, tell her that all our dear Sisters and I are praying for her. I am asking the good Lord and the Most Holy Virgin to please spare her for the sake of her children. I would willingly sacrifice my life to Our Lord in her place if it were not contrary to his will.

The sacraments do not kill anyone; they tell me that my aunt began her confession, which pleased me. I hope that she completed it and that she will have the joy of receiving Our Lord, who alone can heal the soul and the body. Tell her that I am often by her side in thought and ask my little niece to kiss her mother for me.

Since I am unable to send the medal my aunt asked for, I am sending her a small piece of cloth from the Holy Father's cassock.

Send me news as soon as possible. I close, my beloved sister, with an affectionate kiss. Let us meet at the foot of the Cross, where we will find strength and courage.

Sister Marie-Bernard Soubirous

"Let us thank God for allowing our dear father to receive the last Sacraments."

(To her little brother, Pierre, who was a pensioner at Garaison Junior High School, some time after March 1871)

With both of their parents deceased, Bernadette felt an even greater sense of responsibility for Pierre, her eleven-and-a-half-year-old little brother and godson. She comforted and encouraged him, guided him spiritually and advised him about what his behavior and his attitude should be in school at Garaison.

This letter comes from a copy that is in the archives in Nevers; hence, there is no signature.

My Dear Little Pierre,

I was very happy with your little letter and especially with your good mood. You seem full of desire to please your dear and worthy teacher. My good little friend, continue doing your best to respond generously to his care and his paternal concern. God will bless you for it. You will be a consolation to me if you are pious and obedient and if you work hard, as you said in your letter. I ask Our Lord and the Most Holy Virgin to help you in this way every day.

I am sure that you must have been deeply grieved by the loss of our beloved father, who was taken away from us so suddenly. How fortunate it was that you saw him a few days before his death. What a consolation for you and for our poor father! I thank God for it. Let us also thank God for allowing our dear father to receive the last sacraments. My dear little Pierre, let us pray often for the repose of his soul, for our dear mother and for our dear Aunt Lucile, whom God also called to himself. Remember our good sister Marie in your prayers. She needs courage and good health to take care of her little boy. Her mother's heart has suffered so much from the loss of her little Bernadette.

I have not heard from Jean-Marie in a long time, so I am writing him.

Adieu, my dear little Pierre. Give my sincere regards to Father Superior and ask him to remember me in his holy prayers.

Affectionate kisses, my little friend.

Your devoted sister.

"Let us pray for each other that Our Lord may give us the grace that we need to become saints."

(To her brother, Jean-Marie, a postulant at the novitiate of the Brothers of Ploërmel, some time after March 1871)

From March to May 1871, Paris was asunder because of the Commune, a serious civil uprising. By the end of May, revolutionaries were threatening to burn and pillage religious sites in Nevers, especially Saint-Gildard and the bishop's residence.

On June 27, following his novitiate, Brother Marie-Bernard was sent to study in Eauze. Three years later, following his mandatory military service, he left religious life permanently without telling Bernadette.

This letter lacks both a salutation and a signature. It comes from a copy of the original.

I come to you today to kiss the crosses that our divine Master has sent us. Let us ask him for the grace to carry them according to his example, obediently and generously.

Our trials this year have been great, have they not, dear brother? Three members of our family have been taken away from us in the space of a few days. The good Lord has his plans, it is true, but it has been a hard blow. Our poor father was taken from us so suddenly. We had the consolation of knowing that he received the last sacraments. It is a great grace for which we should thank God. Nevertheless, dear friend, let us pray for the repose of his soul and for our good Aunt Lucile, whose children are to be greatly pitied. Please pray to the Holy

Virgin also for our sister Marie, who surely needs it; you know how much she has suffered from losing her little Bernadette whom she loved so much. What a great sorrow for a mother!

I am including a letter for our little Pierre, who wrote me such a sweet letter.

Dear brother, write me soon. I am worried about you.

Give my regards to your Director and ask him and the Community to pray for me.

Adieu, my very dear brother. Let us pray for each other that Our Lord may give us the grace that we need to become saints. Let us be generous in the sacrifices that the good Master sends us and let us offer them for the repose of the souls of those we have lost.

Your very devoted sister.

"Yes, my dear child, you will surely be happy if you love the good Lord who protects you."

(To Bernadette Nicolau, January 1872)

Bernadette Nicolau was the eight-year-old daughter of Saint Berna-dette's Aunt Bernarde (Saint Bernadette's godmother). The little girl was Bernadette's "favorite"; hence, when she referred to herself as "aunt", the term indicated her affection for the child.

My Dearest Child,

Your last letter in which you wished me Happy New Year so beautifully brought me so much pleasure. It shows me that you are thinking about me. Thank you, my dear, for your good wishes; mine for you are just as strong and just as sincere. Always be good and study hard so that you will be sure to make your father and your teachers happy. And I need no more than that to satisfy my heart, which is full of affection for you. Yes, my dear child, you will surely be happy if you love the good Lord who protects you in a special way by allowing you to receive a Christian education. There are so many who do not enjoy the same advantage as you; so thank the Lord and think about the aunt sometimes who often thinks about you, her favorite.

My health is not as bad as last year, but this winter's bitter cold has made me a little ill. I am having a little trouble breathing, but don't worry about me and tell the family not to worry either.

Adieu, my dear little child. I send you affectionate kisses.

Tell your excellent teachers that I send them good wishes for the New Year.

Your aunt who loves you.[9]

[9] This is the only signature on the original letter.

"Let us pray hard for these poor sinners to be converted. They are our brothers, after all!"

(To Mother Alexandrine Roques, April 3, 1872)

J. M. J.   Nevers, April 3, 1872

My Dearest Mother,

Let me begin by giving you news of our dear and venerable Mother General, who has been confined to her room for the last three months. As you can imagine, we are all very sad. We spent the month of Saint Joseph asking for her to be healed. Evidently we did not pray very well since our dear Mother is still sick. There is a little improvement, but not much. Pray to the Most Holy Virgin to grant us this grace, if it be for the greater glory of her divine Son. Nevertheless, I would not want to offend Saint Joseph whom I love so much; then again, they do not get angry in Heaven.

I am waiting impatiently for Mademoiselle Léontine: will she be coming soon? It takes them forever to make a decision in my part of the country!

Dear Mother, let me wish you and all the dear Sisters a joyous Alleluia. We have more to cry about than to rejoice about seeing our poor France so hardened and so blinded. How offended our Lord must be! Let us pray hard for these poor sinners to be converted. They are our brothers, after all! Let us ask Our Lord and the Most Holy Virgin to change these wolves into lambs.

Forget my body, it is fine; but please pray for my poor soul.

Please tell Father Peyramale that I send him my most humble and respectful regards and ask him to remember one of his little lambs in his holy prayers.

Dearest Mother and all the dear Sisters, please accept my most respectful affection.

Your grateful little servant,
Sister Marie-Bernard Soubirous

"I am serious when I ask if you have made a vow not to write me anymore."

(To Brother Marie-Bernard Soubirous, April 1872)

For many years, Bernadette had been trying with difficulty to overcome her "sensitivity". In this letter we see a rare example of her quick temper expressed with sarcasm. The angry tone is underscored in the original French by the use of the formal form of you (vous) instead of the familiar form (tu). When Bernadette did lose her temper, she quickly repented and was often so drained afterwards that on occasion she even fell ill.

This brief letter also allows us to see how much she needed contact with her loved ones. Bernadette was affectionate and loving, and she was frequently disappointed that her siblings did not write her as much as she would have liked. She was far from home and there was no one like her to whom she could confide, no one who had experienced what she had. Her familial attachments were ever the more precious to her because of that, and they were a comfort when she was ill. At times, they were also a source of sorrow.

This fragment comes from an unsigned copy.

Pardon me if I am bothering you, but I am serious when I ask if you have made a vow not to write me anymore. I have been waiting for a letter from you for a year. Considering how much time has passed with no word from you, I finally decided to write and ask you to please let me know you are still alive, if you have not made a vow that is.

Please give my profound respects to Reverend Brother Director and ask him and the Community to pray for me.

"How good Jesus is to ... make of our poor hearts his dwelling place."

(To her brother and godson, Pierre, on his First Communion, May 23, 1872)

My Dear Little Brother,

I was overjoyed to hear that you are going to experience the precious joy of receiving First Communion on the ninth of June. My dear little brother, it goes without saying that from this moment on, your heart, your spirit and your soul should be occupied with one thought alone: preparing your heart to be God's dwelling place. Oh, yes! Our good Savior must continually be present in your thoughts and you must pray to him to prepare his dwelling place himself so nothing is lacking when he arrives. The angels envy your happiness already, they who possess this God three times holy. They sing his praises without ceasing, but they cannot receive him as we do. How good Jesus is to humble himself to give himself to us and to make of our poor hearts his dwelling place. Invoke the Most Holy Virgin, my dear little friend. Ask her to grant you all the graces you need for this great act.

The whole community is praying for you and your classmates. We are especially asking that all of you be faithful and devout Christians, that you love God with all your hearts and most especially that our good Jesus bless you with a horror of all that is evil or that might displease him in any way.

I am so grateful to Father, the Prefect of Discipline, for informing me of the date of your First Communion well in advance. It gave me such happiness. Please extend my profound respects to him.

I remember Mademoiselle Joséphine Cazenave very well; I am delighted to learn that she is a Religious. I ask her, as a friend, to please remember me sometimes in her holy prayers.

Dear little friend, do not forget to give my sincere regards to your dear and worthy professor. Please ask him and all those of the Community of Garaison to pray for me.

Thank you, my dear little brother, for remembering me in your prayers and for the prayers of your classmates. And do not forget the souls of our poor deceased parents.

My dear little brother, this letter comes to you with an affectionate kiss.

Adieu, my dear little brother. I will meet you in the Sacred Hearts of Jesus and Mary.

Sister Marie-Bernard Soubirous

Doctor Robert-Saint-Cyr's medical opinion of Sister Marie-Bernard

(From Dr. Pierre Robert-Saint-Cyr to Dr. Damoiseau, September 3, 1872)

Bernadette's story was so well known all over France that almost everyone had an opinion about whether or not the apparitions were genuine, and it was not unusual for so-called experts who had never even met her to make their opinions known publicly. Such was the case with Dr. Voisin of Salpêtrière, a psychiatric hospital in Paris. Dr. Voisin had publicly stated that "the miracle at Lourdes was affirmed on the faith of a child suffering from hallucinations who is confined in an Ursuline Convent in Nevers." Apparently, Dr. Voisin did not even know to which religious order Bernadette belonged.

Dr. Damoiseau, President of the Medical Society of Orne, wanted to know if Dr. Voisin's accusation was true. He wrote to Dr. Pierre Robert-Saint-Cyr, President of the Medical Society of Nièvre and physician to the Sisters at Saint-Gildard, asking for an assessment of Bernadette's medical condition. Dr. Robert-Saint-Cyr knew Bernadette both as a patient and a nurse's aid in the infirmary. The following letter is Dr. Robert-Saint-Cyr's unequivocal response to Dr. Damoiseau's request.

Dear Colleague,

You have come to the right person for the information you want about the young girl from Lourdes, now known as Sister Marie-Bernard. As doctor for the Community, I have been caring for this young Sister for a long time. Her very delicate health has given us reason for concern. At the present time, her health has improved and she has gone from being a patient to becoming my nurse and performing her duties perfectly.

She is a small, rather sickly-looking, twenty-seven-year-old woman. She has a calm and gentle nature, and she cares for her patients with a great deal of intelligence. She carries out every order impeccably; hence, she inspires respect and she has my entire confidence.

As you can see, this young Sister is far from insane. I shall go further: her calm, simple and gentle nature does not dispose her in the least to being susceptible to insanity.

Dear colleague, I am happy for this opportunity to talk with you and to be of assistance by furnishing the information you have requested.

Doctor Robert-Saint-Cyr,
President of the Medical Society of Nièvre

"Remember me when you are close to the Sacred Hearts of Jesus and Mary."

(To her brother Pierre, December 8, 1872)

My Dear Little Brother,

Thank you for the good news about the family; I am especially happy to learn that our cousin Pierre Vignes is with you at Garaison. Both of you please be good, apply yourselves to your schoolwork and love God and the Most Holy Virgin so they will protect us. This is how to please your dear and worthy teacher. My good little friends, continue to respond generously to his care and his paternal concern. God will love you and bless you for it.

I was very happy to read the excellent resolutions you made during the retreat, especially for wanting to love the Good Lord and the Most Holy Virgin with all your heart. That is what I ask for you every day. I would almost like to add this one resolution to yours so that you make the most of your time: "I will also work very hard in class so that I may please Jesus."

Adieu, my dear little Pierre. Please give my profound respects to Father Superior and ask him to remember me in his holy prayers. I thank him with all my heart for all his kindness to you.

My dear friends, I am sending you affectionate kisses. Pray for me that I may become a holy Religious.

Let us also pray for poor sinners, for our Holy Father and for the Holy Church. Let us not forget the dear souls in Purgatory, especially those of our dear parents.

Adieu, my good little brother. Remember me when you are close to the Sacred Hearts of Jesus and Mary; that is where I will meet you.

> Your very devoted sister,
> Sister Marie-Bernard Soubirous

Here is my address:
Sister Marie-Bernard Soubirous
Motherhouse of The Sisters of Charity
Saint-Gildard, Nevers

"My cross became lighter and suffering became sweet when I knew that Jesus was going to be with me."

(To her sister, Marie, April 28, 1873)

On January 17, 1873, the Journal of the Community *recorded the following note: "My Sister Marie-Bernard had a serious asthma attack and was sent to the Sainte-Julienne Infirmary." On February 3, the following entry was made: "Sister Marie-Bernard is very ill." By Easter, April 13, there was a little improvement and she was able to go to Mass. Unfortunately, she had a relapse and spent the following two weeks in bed. When she wrote to family and friends, she was honest, but matter-of-fact about her condition. The seriousness of her illness and her terrible suffering made her faith reaction all the more inspiring: "Our Lord is so good. The entire time I was sick, I had the joy of receiving him in my poor and unworthy heart three times a week."*

My Dear Marie,

I have been anxious to let you know how I am doing. Here I am, resuscitated once again after spending three months in bed. It began with quite a long asthma attack. After that, I started spitting up blood; I could not make the slightest movement without it starting up again. As you can imagine, being nailed down like that did not agree with my lively nature. My strength is returning though and I went to Mass for the first time on Easter.

Our Lord is so good. The entire time I was sick, I had the joy of receiving him in my poor and unworthy heart three times a week. My cross became lighter and suffering became sweet when I knew that Jesus was going to be with me and that I would have the great honor of welcoming him in my heart, he, who comes to suffer with those who suffer, to cry with those who cry. Where can you find a friend like Jesus? He knows how to sympathize with us and how to soothe our pain at the same time. Jesus, and Jesus alone, can do that. Let us love him and cling to him with all our hearts.

Please let me know if Cousin Lucile Nicolau is with the Sisters of the Cross at Saint-Pé. Don't forget. I am very anxious to know. Marie-Bernard[10] wrote me and it seems that Joseph went to see him. I would invite all of you to come visit me, but it is too far. We will see each other again in Heaven, where we will never have to be separated again. Please give my best to all our dear relatives and ask them not to forget me in their prayers. Remember me especially when you go to my dear Grotto. You will find me there sometimes. I go there often, even without permission.

Write as soon as possible and let me know how you are and tell me how little Justine is. Kiss her for me. Adieu, my good sister. Always remember that you have my sincere and religious affection.

Your devoted sister,
Sister Marie-Bernard Soubirous

[10] Bernadette's brother.

"Pray for me to become a Religious according to the heart of Our Lord."

(To Brother Marie-Bernard, May 20, 1873)

The May 12th entry in the Journal of the Community *reported that both Mother Josephine Imbert and Bernadette were improving. They made a short trip to Varennes and Fourchambault. Bernadette was invited to speak to the orphans at Varennes, but she fell ill and was carried back to the carriage by four of the students. On June 3, she received last rites for the third time.*

J. M. J.   Nevers, May 20, 1873

My Dearest Brother,

   I am so very sorry that I was unable to write sooner, but I have been gravely ill. It began with an asthma attack and then I started spitting up blood. The slightest movement made it start up again and I was confined to bed for three months. I attended Mass for the first time on Easter, but I had a small relapse that kept me in bed for another two weeks.

   Don't worry. There is nothing wrong with my lungs. It is something to do with the heart. I could live for a long time, or I could die in my sleep. I have put myself in the hands of Our Lord and the Most Holy Virgin. I am feeling better and I am getting my strength back a little bit. Pray for me.

Please extend my most profound respects to Reverend Brother Director and tell him that I am praying several "O Mary, conceived without sin, etc." for his intentions. I am very happy to think that I am united in prayer with your dear Community.

Please thank Father for remembering me at the altar. I am very grateful to him for it.

Adieu, my dear Brother. Pray for me to become a Religious according to the heart of Our Lord.

Your most devoted sister in the Sacred Hearts of Jesus and Mary.

Sister Marie-Bernard Soubirous

P.S.—Send me all your news as soon as possible.

"Pray less for my health and much more for my poor soul."

(To her cousin, Lucile Pène, May 21, 1873)

My Dearest Cousin,

Thank you for all your prayers and for the prayers of your dear parents. Pray less for my health and much more for my poor soul. Most importantly, ask Our Lord to make me a Religious according to his own heart. I will always be healthy enough, but I will never have enough love for Our Lord.

Please remember me to my uncles and aunts and give them my love.

Tell your little brother to be good and obedient to his Papa and Mama.[11] He needs to behave himself since he is preparing for his First Communion.

Ask Marie to kiss my little Nicolau cousins for me and also little Bernadette Vignes, whom I love so much.

Adieu, dear cousin. Remember me when you are close to the Sacred Hearts of Jesus and Mary.

Your most devoted cousin,

Sister Marie-Bernard Soubirous

"Teach your child to know and love the good Lord and the Most Holy Virgin as soon as possible."

(To her sister, Marie, September 6, 1874)

Marie had already lost three children and, unbeknownst to the family, little Bernadette-Irma was not destined to live much longer either.

My Good Marie,

I was so pleased to learn that both you and your little girl are in good health. Ask Our Lord and the Most Holy

---

[11] Lucile and her brother were the children of Bernadette's Aunt Basile.

Virgin to watch over this dear child whom I love so much. Marie, as much as I want her to be healthy, I would prefer a thousand times over to learn that she had died than to find out some day that she was not a good Christian. You understand the care that you must take in bringing up this dear child. Teach her to know and love the good Lord and the Most Holy Virgin as soon as possible, to respect you and to abhor evil; by doing this, you will fulfill your responsibilities as parents. Do not forget that one day Our Lord will ask you to account for this dear soul.

Please give all my love to my godmother and her family. Every day, I ask Our Lord and the Most Holy Virgin to help them to be good and to love God. Yes, children, love God well during this life. This is the greatest source of happiness on this earth and the only thing that will make us eternally happy in Heaven.

Remember me to Aunt Basile, Uncle Jean-Marie and their families. Once again, all my love to all of you.

My good sister, try to find out if Marie-Bernard is still at Eauze. I am very unhappy with him. I have written him twice without receiving an answer. Thank Joseph for writing. I am so very pleased that he has been doing his schoolwork so faithfully. It is truly the greatest consolation he can give me.

I cannot answer the letter that was attached to yours because we are only permitted to write to family.

Remember me in your prayers, especially when you go to my dear Grotto.

Kiss your little Bernadette[12] for me. I was very happy to hear that she is so well behaved.

---

[12] Marie's first daughter, Marie-Bernard, had also been called Bernadette.

I shall close now, my good Marie, with an affectionate kiss for you and your dear little girl.

> Your most devoted sister in the
> Sacred Hearts of Jesus and Mary,
>
> Sister Marie-Bernard Soubirous

"How blind man is when he refuses to open his heart to the light of faith!"

(To her sister, Marie, July 4, 1875)

The flood of 1875 was catastrophic; fortunately, all of Bernadette's relatives escaped harm. Her "dear Grotto" had indeed been flooded for twenty-four hours; however, there was no damage to the Grotto, the esplanade or the construction site.

The little girl whom Marie was supposed to kiss for Bernadette was Marie's daughter Bernadette-Irma who was then fifteen months old. Their brother Pierre was fifteen. Jean-Marie was still in the military and it was highly unlikely that he would return to religious life.

When Saint Bernadette was a baby, her mother was unable to nurse her, so the child was sent to live with a wet nurse, Marie Aravant Laguës, in Bartès. For the rest of her life, Bernadette referred to Madame Laguës as her "nanny". During the winter of 1857, there was not enough food for everyone in the Soubirous home, so Bernadette returned to live with the Laguës family. In Bartès, she tended the sheep. Madame Laguës was supposed to be teaching Bernadette the catechism so that she would be able to receive First Communion; unfortunately, she found this task so frustrating that she finally told Bernadette: "You will never learn anything!" and she threw the catechism book across the room. It was Bernadette's ardent desire to learn the catechism and to receive First Communion that led to her determination to return to the family home fifteen days before the first apparition on February 11, 1858. (The poverty-stricken family had been reduced to living in a one-room former prison cell that had been condemned as too unhealthy and uninhabitable for prisoners.)

My Dear Sister,

I have heard that the Gave has flooded and I am extremely worried. I am anxious to know if the Grotto and the mills along the banks of the river have been damaged. As for the town, it looks as though there is nothing to worry about. Evidently, the flood did a great deal of damage in Tarbes and Bagnères and there were even some deaths. I am very worried about our relatives in Momères. Try to let me know how they are as soon as possible.

Our cousin Jeanne wrote me from the Trappist Motherhouse and asked me to remember her to you and our brothers. I am very worried about her being so close to Toulouse, where the flood caused such devastation. According to what I have heard, the number of people swallowed up by the water is incalculable. No one has ever seen anything like this.

God does punish us, but always as a Father. The streets of Paris have been washed in the blood of so many victims,[13] yet this was not enough to touch hearts hardened by evil. The streets of the South had to be washed too with

---

[13] This is a reference to the Commune of 1871.

even more deaths. My God! How blind man is when he refuses to open his heart to the light of faith! After such disasters, will we not be tempted to ask ourselves what could have provoked such terrible punishments? If we listen carefully, we will hear a voice deep within our hearts saying to us that it is sin, yes, sin, since sin is the greatest disaster and it is the cause of every punishment. The evil that we commit maliciously comes back to us; such is the joy and the profit we receive from sinful acts.

My good Marie, please be my interpreter with all my dear relatives, uncles, aunts and cousins and give them my love. Give your little girl a big kiss from me. So she has been sick? Let me know how she is, and my two brothers too, as soon as possible. What has Pierre been doing lately? He has been very lazy about writing me. I do not know what to think about Jean-Marie. He has not written me in such a long time. Please tell him not to leave me in the dark about him. When you see my good nanny,[14] give her and her children all my best.

Our dear Sister Nathalie said you are thinking of coming to see me. Believe me, dear friend, I would certainly be very happy to see you, as well as my brothers. On the other hand, it is so far that, if by chance something unfortunate happened to you on the way, I would reproach myself for it for the rest of my life.

Adieu, my dear Marie.

Your sister who sends you a kiss,

Sister Marie-Bernard Soubirous

---

[14] Marie Aravant Laguës of Bartès. There is no entirely accurate translation for the French word *nourrice* in this context. It means "nanny, wet nurse, baby sitter". In this context, it refers to the former childhood relationship.

CHAPTER 6

The "White Chapel"
1875–1879

By October 1875, Bernadette was truly an invalid. She was confined to her bed, or what she called her "White Chapel"; henceforth, her "job is to be sick", she said. It would not be until July 1876 that she would even be able to attend Sunday Mass. For Bernadette, this was the greatest hardship of all.

Before he left for Rome, Monsignor de Ladoue, Bishop of Nevers, visited Saint-Gildard and asked Bernadette to write Pope Pius IX to ask for his apostolic blessing. She was mortified at the thought that she, "a poor Sister", should write to His Holiness; nevertheless, she did so through obedience. Not only did her humility and lack of education make this an overwhelming task, she was so ill that she needed to write the letter from her sick-bed while another Sister steadied a little wooden lap desk for her. In January 1877, the Bishop returned to Saint-Gildard and announced that His Holiness: "in response to the letter of Sister Marie-Bernard, sends to her in particular and to the entire Congregation a blessing signed by his own hand."

These years ushered in more deaths that affected Bernadette profoundly. In 1878, Marie's fourth child, Bernadette-Irma, died at eighteen months of age and the following year, Lucie-Françoise, Marie's fifth child, died at eighteen months, the same tender age as her sister. In July 1877, Monsignor de Ladoue, Bishop of Nevers, died at the end of a Mass he was celebrating. Perhaps most heartbreaking of all for Bernadette, Monsignor Peyramale,[1] *her former pastor and faithful source of support in Lourdes, who had been with her since the beginning, died unexpectedly on September 7, 1877. Finally, in early 1878, His Holiness Pope Pius IX and Mother Imbert both passed on.*

During Bernadette's final year of life, Father Cros began to exert great pressure on the Sisters of Nevers to give him permission to interrogate her for his book on her life and the apparitions. Bernadette reminded her superiors of their promise not to subject her to such questioning anymore and Mother General rejected Father Cros' request. Nevertheless, he continued to pressure the bishop, and he finally received permission to send multiple questionnaires. The effort to comply exhausted the terminally ill young woman, and one must assume that it took an emotional toll as well. In addition to Father Cros' questionnaires, during the last months of her life Bernadette recounted the events of Massabielle for Church authorities one final time. This proved exhausting and she began to question her memory, saying that if she inadvertently contradicted herself, they should accept her initial accounts. Not only was she ill and exhausted, but the details that were important to her were not necessarily the same as those that seemed so essential to her interrogators.

On September 22, 1878, Bernadette was allowed to make her perpetual vows; she referred to them affectionately as her "great vows". During this same year, her brother, Jean-Marie, visited her at Saint-Gildard. The Sisters carried her downstairs in an arm-

---

[1] In recognition of Father Peyramale's service to the Church, on March 3, 1874, Pope Pius IX signed a brief that made him a prothonotary apostolic, which granted him the title Monsignor. Although both archbishops and bishops are called Monsignor in France, Monsignor Peyramale was not elevated to the rank of bishop. A prothonotary apostolic is a priest of the chief college of the papal curia who keeps records of consistories and canonizations and signs papal bulls. Monsignor Peyramale was made an honorary member of this college.

chair to see him, and the long-separated brother and sister had a lengthy, emotional last visit. One month before her death, Marie, her beloved sister, and Marie's husband Joseph made their first and last visit to Bernadette at the Convent.

On March 28, 1879, Bernadette again received last rites; this time they truly were last rites. On April 16, 1879, at approximately 3:15 P.M., Saint Bernadette rendered up her soul to her beloved Savior and his Mother, the beautiful Lady of her visions.

"Inexhaustible treasures of grace are opened to you through the Eucharist."

(To her young cousins, around 1875)

This beautiful letter expresses the centrality of the Eucharist in Bernadette's spiritual life. It also makes an eloquent statement about how we should prepare our hearts to receive the Eucharist.

(The letter is from an unsigned copy.)

My Dearest Little Cousins,

I was so happy to learn that you will soon experience the precious blessing of making your First Communion. My dear little friends, you can be sure that I am joining my prayers with yours, however weak they may be. I do so with all my heart and so do all our dear Sisters in the Community. Everything about this day should show you how important it is, from the great care they are taking to prepare you for it, to the solemnity with which this beautiful day is always surrounded. Indeed, is there a more sacred or more important act? Inexhaustible treasures of grace are opened to you through the Eucharist and its influence in your lives should increase over the years to come. So pray often. Pray to Our Lord and his Most Holy Mother to help you understand the importance of this great act.

My dear little friends, this sweet day, the object of your desires, so rich in the happiness and holy joy you have heard spoken of so often, will soon arrive. This day will be beautiful, great and solemn. It will fill your young hearts with holy consolations. It will be a precious memory, since, for the first time, you will be given a place at the heavenly banquet, where you will be nourished with the Body of God. You will be washed and your thirst quenched in his Blood, intimately united with his divinity and blessed with the grace of his love.

Ask Jesus, our Savior, to come prepare a place for himself in your young hearts so there will be nothing to grieve him when he arrives. Think only of Jesus, since he is choosing to rest in your souls. Make his dwelling place like a sanctuary of innocence and peace.

O my dear children, we would have to have the hearts of angels to receive Our Lord as he deserves, so try to receive him with as much faith, humility and love as you can. And when Our Lord is in your heart, trust Him completely and dwell in the delights of his presence. Love, worship, listen, praise. Oh, the happy moment! Eternity alone holds greater joys for us.

Take advantage of Our Lord's presence to ask him for all kinds of graces, for yourselves, for your parents, for all those who prepared you for this important act, for the Church, for our Holy Father the Pope, for the dear souls in Purgatory, for poor sinners.

Finally, go to Mary's altar. Confide your resolutions to her and put the treasure of your innocence and devotion under her protection. You know that we never turn to her in vain. Ask her for the grace to love Our Lord as she herself loves him and to remain faithful to him both in life and in death.

Adieu, my dear little cousins. I close by asking you to remember me a little in your prayers.

"Dear friend, you have no idea how interested I am in the welfare of your soul."

(To her brother, Pierre, June 25, 1876)

Bernadette's own education having been so neglected, she was acutely aware of the importance of a good education. In her letters to children, she encouraged them by saying they would be a consolation to her if they were pious and obedient and if they worked hard in school. Bernadette's entire intellectual, spiritual and personal appreciation of education is succinctly summed up in an earlier letter to eight-year-old Bernadette Nicolau: "Always be good and study hard so that you will be sure to make your father and your teachers happy. And I need no more than that to satisfy my heart, which is full of affection for you. Yes, my dear child, you will surely be happy if you love the good Lord who protects you in a special way by allowing you to receive a Christian education. There are so many who do not enjoy the same advantage as you."

Bernadette took great pains to assure that both of her brothers received opportunities that she did not enjoy. Sadly, she perceived that neither was truly taking advantage of the education being provided to them and in this letter she expressed her frustration with Pierre. In addition, it was becoming increasingly clear that neither brother had a religious vocation. This being the case, she advised Pierre on the importance of discerning precisely what his vocation was.

Her repetition of the closing salutation "adieu"[2] reflects her awareness of the seriousness of her illness. She wanted to see Pierre settled while she was still here to help him.

My Dear Pierre,

You are evidently too lazy to write me. Didn't you receive the letter I wrote on February 29th, or is it possible that you have been sick? Please let me know how you are because I have been very worried about you. Have you made a decision about your vocation? What do you plan to do? Dear friend, you have no idea how interested I am in the welfare of your soul. Not a day passes that I do not pray for you to Our Lord and to the Most Holy Virgin to give you discernment about your vocation and to show you God's holy will. This is not the kind of decision we make overnight; it is for the rest of our lives and usually our eternal happiness depends on our vocation. So pray much, dear friend, that God will show you the choice you should make, both for love of him and for your own salvation.

You would not be happy with me if I sent this letter without mentioning my health. I am better and I can attend

---

[2] *Adieu (à Dieu)*, or farewell, implies a lengthy separation. Translated literally, it means "to God", suggesting that reunion will only take place when the two are in Heaven.

holy Mass on Sundays. Keep praying for me. Please give
my respects to Reverend Father Superior. Please ask him
and Reverend Father Sempé to remember me in their holy
prayers.

Adieu, dear brother, I close with a kiss.

Adieu, dear friend. In the Sacred Hearts of Jesus and Mary,

Sister Marie-Bernard Soubirous

"I am able to attend holy Mass on Sunday, which is
a great consolation for me."

(To Mother Alexandrine Roques, June 25, 1876)

*It is often said that invalids become progressively more self-
absorbed, but nothing could be further from the truth for Bernadette. She was "ashamed" to have to admit that she was then so
weak that it took two people to help her reach the choir to attend
Mass, a negligible distance for a person in good health. In the same
letter, although she did ask Mother to work (i.e., pray) for her "a
little since she has been so lazy", her focus was on asking for help
for Sister Claire and the assistant chaplain, both of whom were ill.*

*The assistant chaplain to whom Bernadette referred was Father
Auguste Perreau, an excellent and devout priest who was in ill
health. He celebrated Mass every day at Saint-Gildard. He and
Bernadette prayed for each other's intentions and she was able to
confide in him. She shared her concerns about family issues and
she even told him that she had made "a pact with Our Lord for
sinners". On his first trip to the Grotto for the crowning of the*

statue of the Holy Virgin, he said to the Blessed Mother: "I am here in Bernadette's place." Father Perreau testified in a deposition that among the five or six letters he took to Lourdes for Bernadette, "the first was addressed to the Holy Virgin of the Grotto". Unfortunately, if this letter still exists, its location is unknown.

My Dearest Mother,

How fortunate I am to have the opportunity of sending you news.[3] I am ashamed to have to tell you that I am still in poor health, but I have been feeling better for the last few days. I am able to attend holy Mass on Sunday, which is a great consolation for me, especially after having been deprived of this great grace for such a long time. I am still not very strong and it takes two people to help me rather than one. It is a little humiliating, but what can I do? I must accept it since it is God's will.

Our little organist, Sister Claire, is my companion in the infirmary. She is extremely ill with a very serious respiratory condition. I promised her that you and the dear Sisters would pray a novena to Our Lady of Lourdes for her. It made her so happy and she thanks you in advance. The Community is beginning the novena tonight, but we are counting on you to continue it. We want the Holy Virgin to heal her so much. She is so lovely and a little angel of piety.

Dearest Mother, you will soon be receiving the latest news of the Community in person from Sister Melanie's sisters, who were recently here visiting, and from our assistant chap-

[3] The opportunity to which she referred was that she was sending the letter with Sister Mélanie's sisters. They had been visiting and were returning to Lourdes.

lain, who is coming to Lourdes for his health. I recommend him to you and to Father Pomian. He is very shy. Knowing how ill he is, we are afraid he may be forced to stop before ever reaching Lourdes like last time. It breaks my heart, knowing how much he has longed to make this trip. I hope the Holy Virgin will grant him this grace.

Dearest Mother, I long to hear from you and our dear Sisters. I know how busy you are, especially now, so I am praying for all of you in a special way. But I hope that you will work a little for me too since I have been lazy for so long.

Please give my kindest, most grateful and respectful regards to Monsignor Peyramale and Father Pomian and ask them to remember me in their holy prayers.

Dearest Mother and dear Sisters, I remain your most grateful, affectionate and obedient child.

Sister Marie-Bernard Soubirous

"I am still in my white chapel."

(To Sister Victorine Poux, June 27, 1876)

Bernadette called her bed in the infirmary her "white chapel". There would have been about seven to nine beds per room in the infirmary. Each bed had a long stretch of white material suspended from the ceiling that draped over the head and foot of the bed. This created a canopy that provided a small degree of privacy and some protection from drafts. Bernadette had adorned her canopy with holy cards, hence the affectionate term: her "white chapel".

In spite of the fact that she was so severely ill and incapacitated that she was carried to Mass, her prayer request had nothing to do with her health. Instead, her concern was for her soul: "May I finally be converted once and for all."

My Dearest Sister Victorine,

I am delighted to have the opportunity to send this letter with Sister Mélanie's sisters. These good ladies are happy to take this letter to you and the dear Sisters.

What can I say about my[4] ... ? I am still in my white chapel. For the last three weeks, however, I have been able to attend holy Mass on Sunday, although it means I have to go back to bed afterward. I have completely lost the use of my legs. I have to undergo the humiliation of being carried, but our Sisters do it with such kind hearts that it truly makes the sacrifice less difficult. I am always afraid they will hurt themselves. When I tell them that, they start laughing, almost making fun of me, and say they could carry four like me.

Please offer my profound respects to Father Pomian and tell him that I need his prayers in a very special way right now, and yours too. I truly need them! May I finally be converted once and for all.

I would be very grateful to Father Pomian if he would take our assistant chaplain[5] under his protection a little bit. He is very shy and quite ill. I know Father's charity too well to be afraid to ask him for this favor.

[4] Illegible word, but very likely "health".
[5] The assistant chaplain was Father Perreau.

I send all my affection and respect to you, all of our dear Sisters and Mother Philomène and her companions. Ask the dear little orphans to pray a Hail Mary for me. I am praying for them.

These ladies will give you a package. Would you please give it to Marie? Thank you for all your kindness to me and my loved ones.

Your obedient and affectionate Sister,

Sister Marie-Bernard Soubirous

"I especially beseech you to be faithful to your Christian obligations. That will be your source of strength and light in all your sorrows and difficulties."

(To her brother, Jean-Marie,[6] July 1, 1876)

At long last, Bernadette heard from her beloved brother, Jean-Marie, but she was too ill to respond immediately. When she was finally able to write, she was warm and affectionate. Her gentle but firm advice to her siblings and the concern she expressed for their spiritual welfare betrays the depth of the anxiety she felt for them. Jean-Marie was released from his military duty on November 11, 1876, but Bernadette had serious doubts about his intention to return to religious life.

[6] Bernadette had good reason to believe that Jean-Marie did not intend to return to the Brothers of Christian Instruction, so from this point on he is referred to by his baptismal name rather than by the name he took in religious life, Brother Marie-Bernard.

My Dear Brother,

I wish I could have answered your letter sooner. It brought me such pleasure, especially since I had not heard from you for so long. I must admit that I was very hurt by your silence and I did not know what to make of it. Dear friend, I hope you will not make me wait so long this time. Please try to make a little bit of an effort.

In his letter, cousin Nicolau said that you are going to be discharged[7] this year. What are your plans? You know that I am just as interested in you when you are far away as when you are near. If I ask you, please understand that it is not mere curiosity. No, dear friend, since we no longer have our parents, it seems to me that it is my responsibility as your[8] older sister to watch out for you.[9] I cannot express how much I care about all three of you. I confess that, at the moment, I am very concerned about your future and about Pierre's future. Every day I pray to Our Lord and the Most Holy Virgin to give you discernment. I especially beseech you to be faithful to your Christian obligations. That will be your source of strength and light in all your sorrows and difficulties. I know there is much that soldiers must suffer in silence. If upon rising every morning they made a point of saying these simple words to Our Lord: "My God, may everything I do and suffer today be for love of you", what treasures they would lay up in eternity. A soldier who is as faithful to his Christian obligations as possible would have as much merit as a Religious. Indeed, the Religious can only hope for any reward for his work and

---

[7] From his mandatory military service.

[8] Bernadette used the plural form of "your" to indicate she felt responsible for all her siblings.

[9] "You" in the plural in French.

his suffering inasmuch as he will have suffered and worked to please Our Lord.

If I have taken so long to answer your letter, please do not think that it was from a lack of interest. No, the only thing that kept me from writing was my usual state of bad health. I am much better now and I have been able to attend holy Mass for the past three weeks. I hope to regain my strength when the weather improves. I have not heard anything from home since I received your letter.

Adieu, my good brother, I close with an affectionate kiss and encouragement to you always to be a good man.

Your sister who loves you always,

Sister Marie-Bernard Soubirous

"My dearest friend, his heart is the only place where you will find true and lasting consolation."

(To Rachel Dufo, July 18, 1876)

Rachel Dufo's father was an attorney and the mayor of Lourdes. Rachel married the very devout Louis-Joseph-Ernest Labbé, who died in 1876. This sorrow was not the only one Rachel experienced at such a young age. Their son, Paul, died at the age of eighteen months and their daughter, Marie, died at the age of six. After the death of her husband, Rachel became a Dominican nun.

Bernadette and Rachel had received their First Communion together; nevertheless, in spite of their early friendship in Lourdes, the social distance between them was still enormous. Rachel used the familiar tu *(you) with Bernadette, but Bernadette used the formal* vous *(you). In a letter dated July 3, 1876, Rachel asked Bernadette to use* tu. *It is reasonable to surmise that Bernadette felt unworthy to do so.*

In her efforts to console her friend, Bernadette quoted Mathew 11:28, albeit with some changes: "Come unto me all ye who labor and are heavy laden and I will give you rest" became "All who suffer and are in pain, come to me. I will soothe you and console you." The changes are slight, but they are meaningful. Not only do they reflect her friend's situation and needs, they also reflect her own at that time. "Labor" and "heavy laden" become "suffer" and "in pain", while "rest" is replaced by "soothe" and "console".

My Good and Dearest Rachel,

I did not expect that such sad circumstances would be the source of my happiness in hearing from you today. Your grief is entirely understandable and reasonable. I cannot begin to tell you how very sorry I am for your loss. God tests those he loves, so you have a very special right to a place in his divine Heart. My dearest friend, his heart is the only place where you will find true and lasting consolation. He himself invites you with those sweet words: "All who suffer and are in pain, come to me. I will soothe you and console you."

Dear friend, seek out our divine Comforter as often as you can; he alone can understand a soul in desolation. Dear friend, you may be assured that you will not be forgotten in my prayers to Our Lord and the Most Holy Virgin, however feeble my prayers may be. Neither will I forget the soul of your dear husband, in whose honor I received Holy Communion. Even in your darkest moments of grief, always remember that you have the greatest of all consolations, and I thank the Lord for it: your dear husband was devout. He left you in the peace and the love of Our Lord. So he whom you mourn is not dead, dear friend, he is only asleep. You will see him in Heaven again, I hope, where there will be no more separation.

I was extremely moved and consoled reading a few lines from one of his letters in which his faith was expressed so beautifully. I am not surprised by the calm and the resignation, I would even go so far as to say the holy indifference his great soul felt at the end about whether he lived or died. It is only the grace of Our Lord that can work such wonders.

Dear friend, let us hope with a firm hope that he whom you mourn is rejoicing or will soon rejoice in the presence of the almighty God who strengthened his soul so often and whom he loved.

How much Our Lord must love you, to afflict you so! Dear friend, I implore you, do not allow yourself to be overcome by grief. Always be obedient and resigned, as you are, to God's will. When we respond this way in faith, Jesus takes possession of hearts so much that he alones acts in us, and this is always sweet, even in the midst of sacrifice. In the depths of your heart, he is sure to speak these words to you: "Courage. I break the dearest bonds on earth, but I reunite them in Heaven. I afflict, but in return, I give myself entirely. I offer myself to you and I take you for my own, you belong to me, I reign in your heart. Courage, my daughter, the cross is the inheritance my friends love best. Here below, suffering; in Heaven, true happiness."

I have not received your last letter or the photograph you mentioned.

Please give my regards to your sister and to her dear daughter.

Dear friend, please remember me a little in your prayers. I would be so grateful if you would say a prayer for me to the Most Holy Virgin, our good Mother, when you go to the Grotto. I shall try to repay you.

Adieu, dear friend. I hope you will not be offended, but I simply could not bring myself to use *tu* with you.

Your friend who loves you in Our Lord and who will meet you in the Sacred Hearts of Jesus and Mary,

Sister Marie-Bernard Soubirous

"For me, to be able to follow the rule of my dear Community is true happiness."

(To her goddaughter, Bernadette Nicolau, August 26, 1876)

In this letter addressed to her thirteen-year-old goddaughter, Bernadette Nicolau, Bernadette provided a health report to her own godmother, but she was insistent that her sister, Marie, not be told how ill she was. She wanted to protect Marie, who had lost yet another of her children, her dear little daughter Bernadette.

My Dearest Bernadette,

Thank you for the good news about the family. I am happy to know that you are all enjoying good health. I ask Our Lord to continue to protect you.

Ask my dear Godmother not to worry about me. I am a little better these days. I am not very sick; it is only that I am very weak. I cannot keep food down; that is why it is taking me so long to regain my strength. I am feeling better, so please do not worry. They take care of me like a little baby. I am truly embarrassed about how kind our venerable Mother General is to me, not to mention how well the nurse takes care of me. All the dear Sisters are wonderful to me. They often tell me that they wish each of them could take a little of my illness on herself so that I could run like before. It makes me laugh to have to tell them that for the moment my greatest source of suffering is that I cannot do the same things they do. For me, to be able to follow the rule of my dear Community is true happiness.

Rest assured, my dear Godmother, I did not forget you or my dear goddaughter before Our Lord and the Most Holy Virgin on your feast days. I hope that will be of some consolation.

Please do not say anything to my sister about my being ill.

Adieu, dear goddaughter. I close with affectionate kisses for all of you. Please remember me in your prayers.

Sister Marie-Bernard Soubirous

"The almighty hand of God . . . strikes only to heal us and make us see the emptiness of the things in this valley of tears where we are only passing through."

(To her sister, Marie, August 26, 1876)

Marie and Joseph Sabathé were mourning the death of their fourth and last child, little Bernadette, who died on August 12, 1876.

Bernadette did what she could to console her sister, first by acknowl-
edging the magnitude of the grief that Marie was suffering, and
second by reminding her sister that "we are only passing through
. . . this valley of tears." These are not platitudes; rather, they are
the deeply held beliefs of a young Religious who had suffered and
who shared her sister's grief. Bernadette spared Marie the knowl-
edge of her own deteriorating health with the simple statement:
"My health is no worse." At the same time, she hinted at the
truth, although it was perhaps an unconscious admission. When
speaking of how many of their loved ones were in Heaven, she
added a cryptic aside: "Perhaps we shall share their joy in a short
while."

My Dear Sister,

Let us always worship and bless the almighty hand of
God. It strikes only to heal us and make us see the emptiness of the things in this valley of tears where we are only
passing through.

I understand that for a mother's heart it is so sad, even
cruel, to lose her fourth child. It is true that the trial is
harsh, but when I see with the eyes of faith, I cannot help
but say with joy: happy the mother who sends angels to
Heaven who will pray for her and for all the family. They
will be our protectors along with Our Lord and the Most
Holy Virgin.

I love to imagine this dear little group in Heaven praying
for us, poor exiles in this valley of tears. Have courage.
Our family is more numerous in Heaven than on earth. Let
us pray, work and suffer as much as pleases the Lord. Perhaps we shall share their joy in a short while.

My good and dear Marie, you and Joseph must be calm. Do not allow yourselves to be overcome by grief. Please let me know how you are doing. I am truly impatient to know. Our venerable Mother General wants me to tell you that she and all the dear Sisters share your grief and they are praying for you.

My health is no worse. It seems there was a rumor that I had died . . .

(Please do not believe anything you hear unless you receive a letter from Nevers.)

Adieu, dear Marie.

> Your sister who kisses you with all her heart,
>
> Sister Marie-Bernard Soubirous

"My hand is trembling like an old lady's."

(To Sister Mathilde Pomian, September 7, 1876)

Sister Mathilde Pomian, Father Pomian's niece, entered religious life at Saint-Gildard on May 26, 1872, at the age of nineteen, and after her profession, she was sent to Provins. In this letter, Bernadette was thanking her for the good news that Father Pomian, Bernadette's former confessor, was planning to visit Saint-Gildard in the near future. Sister Hélène was Sister Hélène Petitcoup, the sacristan.

My Good Sister Mathilde,

Thank you for the good news. As you can imagine, it will be so good to see your dear uncle again. I owe him so much for all that he has done and continues to do for me. I can assure you that I never expected such happy news. There is only one thing I regret and it is that I am not strong enough to take a walk with him. I am still in the infirmary. I am not very sick, but I feel so weak. I have never experienced anything like this. I cannot keep any food down; that is why it is taking me so long to get back on my feet this time. What can I do but be patient and keep saying: *Fiat!*

There are not any dear Sisters from Lourdes at the retreat. I would be so grateful if you would say a little prayer for my poor sister who has just lost her little girl. She seems terribly sad, although she is resigned to it.

Please give my respects to your dear Mother. I was sorry to hear that she is ill. In my feeble prayers, I am asking Our Lord and the Most Holy Virgin to heal her. I beg her to give me a small share in her suffering.

Our venerable Mother General's health is holding up, even though she is a little tired from so much work because of the retreat. Keep praying for God to strengthen her. Dear Sister Hélène comes to the infirmary only rarely, so I have not been able to give her your message.

Adieu, dear friend. I have to close because my hand is shaking like an old lady's. Please give my respects to our dear Sisters and ask them to remember me in their holy prayers. Pray for me. I am praying for you.

Once again, adieu. Your Sister and friend who will meet you in the Sacred Hearts of Jesus and Mary,

Sister Marie-Bernard Soubirous

(The following letter was attached to the preceding.)

Accompanying this letter is an image of the cross with a banderole and the inscription: "Today on the cross and tomorrow in Heaven." On the back, there is a prayer by Mother Marie-Laurence of the Visitation. Bernadette inscribed the following words on the top: "Union in prayer and sacrifice", and on the bottom: "To my dear friend, Rachel Dufo. Sister Marie-Bernard Soubirous, September 13, 1876."

My Dearest Rachel,

This is just a note to tell you that it is with pleasure and gratitude that I accept the little bargain you proposed. Your dear letter gave me such pleasure. Thank you for the decade of the Rosary you will pray for me every day. Ask Our Lord and the Most Holy Virgin especially for the grace of a good death.

Please give my respects to Madame Capdevielle. Tell her that I share in her grief and I am praying for her.

Adieu. I will stop now since I cannot hold the pen any longer and I am not quite sure what I am saying.

Once more, adieu. I shall meet you in the Sacred Hearts of Jesus and Mary.

Your most devoted friend,

Sister Marie-Bernard Soubirous

"I am happier with my Christ than a queen on her throne."

(To Mother Sophie Cresseil, September 21, 1876)

When Mother Sophie Cresseil sent Bernadette a statue of Christ, she had no way of knowing how much it meant to the suffering young nun and how much she had been wanting one.

J. M. J.   Nevers, September 21, 1876

My Dear and Worthy Mother Sophie,[10]

I do not know how to thank you for the beautiful statue of Christ you sent me. It was so kind of you. I am extremely grateful, I assure you. I simply cannot tell you the joy I felt when I saw it. I have wanted a large statue of Christ to put beside my bed for so long. When I saw it, I held it and kissed it and said: "My dear Mother Sophie was truly inspired." I have permission to keep it. Even though I am confined to bed, I am happier with my Christ than a queen on her throne.

Dearest Mother, since I do not know how to express my gratitude, I look at the image of Jesus Crucified as often as possible and pray that he will bless you more and more, as well as all those who work with you.

My dear Mother, allow me to ask you and all our dear Sisters to remember me in your holy prayers. I will not forget you in mine, even though they are so feeble. A spe-

[10] "Dear and Worthy" was the official title given to the Superiors of the Congregation.

cial little ... (*illegible word*) from me to my very dear Sister Nathalie.

Most worthy Mother, you have my most profound respect and gratitude.

Sister Marie-Bernard Soubirous

"Our Lord tells us to seek first the Kingdom of God and everything else will be given to us in abundance."

(To her sister, Marie, November 1876)

In this letter to her sister, Marie, Bernadette made an interesting spelling error in which she unconsciously described her spiritual state. She intended to say: "Remember that Our Lord tells us to seek first the Kingdom of God and everything else will be given to us in abundance." Writing in French, she said: "tout le reste nous sera donné par sur-croix*", meaning "everything else will be given to us* on the cross*", rather than the correct:* surcroît *(in abundance).*

Bernadette had every reason to be hurt; in spite of all that she had done to help her brothers receive an education, neither of them told her directly about their intention not to continue their studies. Neither chose to be a Religious or a priest. It is perhaps difficult for us to realize the challenges this family of a famous visionary and saint must surely have faced. Unlike their sister, they were not favored with intimate conversations with the Holy Virgin.

My Good Sister,

I am surprised that I have not heard from you more often since Pierre moved in. What is he doing? Please let me know if he intends to return to Garaison. He is at an age when he should learn a trade if he is sure he does not have a religious vocation. He needs to make a decision. I do not want him to spend his time running from one thing to another.

Our venerable Mother General said that you are thinking of coming to see me. It is entirely up to you; the only thing I ask is that you write before you leave. Thank you for the kind package you sent with Father Pomian. Dear friend, I hope that you and Joseph are not neglecting your religious obligations. Above all, do everything you can to serve God well. Remember, Our Lord tells us to seek first the Kingdom of God and everything else will be given to us in abundance.

Please give my affection and respect to my good nanny.[11] I was sorry to hear that her dear husband had died. Try to give me her address so I can write her.

Do not forget to offer my profound respects to my dear Mother and all the dear Sisters and ask them to pray for me.

Adieu, my good sister. I close with an affectionate kiss.

Your devoted sister,

Sister Marie-Bernard Soubirous

---

[11] Bernadette meant Marie Aravant Laguës.

"Please keep Sunday holy."

(To her cousin, Lucile Pène, November 3, 1876)

After the apparitions, Bernadette was utterly scrupulous about her behavior and she never accepted money or gifts from pilgrims. Because of the great grace she had received from the Queen of Heaven, she felt an enormous sense of responsibility to live an exemplary Christian life. She understood that her family members had been given an exceptional opportunity to serve as good examples to others because all eyes were on them; she also believed that if they profitted inappropriately from her renown, they offered a dangerous example to others.

My Dearest Cousin,

Your letter brought me such pleasure, and I would have answered sooner if I had not been so ill. I am a little better, but I still cannot leave the infirmary.

Dear cousin, I was deeply troubled to learn that you have to remind your husband that he should go to Mass on Sunday. I tremble for you when I think that Our Lord tells us to seek first the Kingdom of God and his justice. He promises that everything else will be given to us in abundance.[12] Please keep Sunday holy. You will not get rich by working on Sunday. On the contrary, you will bring misfortune on yourselves and your children. For goodness sake, do not do

[12] As in the previous letter, Bernadette wrote *sur-croix* (on the cross) instead of *surcroît* (in abundance).

that! You should be an example, not only for the towns-people, but for strangers who visit Lourdes.

Please give my respects to my dear uncle and aunts and my godmother.

I beseech all my cousins to be faithful to their religious obligations. I ask all of you to pray for me to the Holy Virgin whenever you go to the Grotto.

Adieu, dear friend.

Your cousin who kisses you most affectionately,

Sister Marie-Bernard Soubirous

P.S. Please take my letters to Marie and my brother Pierre as soon as possible. Adieu.

"My advice is to calm down and, most of all, keep the peace and unity that is the source of happiness in a family."

(To her brother, Jean-Marie, ca. November 31, 1876)

Jean-Marie had completed his military service and, much to Bernadette's disappointment, he had decided not to return to the Brothers of Christian Instruction. Back in the family home in Lourdes, he was having difficulty getting along with his sister and brother-in-law; however, the estate could not be settled until Pierre was of age. In spite of the geographic distance, Jean-Marie appealed to Bernadette, the eldest, to help solve family squabbles. She calmed him down, gave him excellent advice and reassured him that when he did get "carried away", he had a safe place to express his emotions. She "will not talk to anyone about what" he has told her in his letters.

My Dear Brother,

I was sad to read in your last letter how unhappy you are with our brother-in-law and our sister. I think you are getting a little carried away. You should not speak or write when you are so upset. Calm down and think first, and then act. Marie has not said anything at all about it, neither about the rock nor the mill. It is impossible to settle anything until Pierre is of age. My advice is to calm down and, most of all, keep the peace and unity that is the source of happiness in a family. Don't worry; I shall not talk to anyone about what you tell me in your letters.

I have not received a letter from the house since August. Pierre wrote to tell me that our dear little niece had died, and Marie has been extremely sad since the death of that dear child. That is how life is: sorrow and sacrifices, all of which should make us see that happiness is not of this world.

What can I tell you about myself? My health is a little better, but I must take many precautions to protect myself from the cold, which is extremely bad for me. Don't worry. I am quite warm here in the infirmary, where the Sister waits on me hand and foot. All the dear Sisters are so extremely kind to me that it is almost embarrassing.

Please do not forget your religious obligations. Remember that where there's a will, there's a way. I am anxious to hear from you, so write as soon as possible.

Adieu, dear friend. Your devoted sister who kisses you most affectionately,

Sister Marie-Bernard Soubirous

"I would not want you to become a priest just to make a position for yourself for anything in the world."

(To her brother, Pierre, November 3, 1876)

As was the case with Jean-Marie, Bernadette was disappointed to learn from a third party that Pierre was not returning to Garaison and did not feel called to religious life. And as always, she did not want her family members to profit from the Grotto. In addition, she understood that her little brother needed a trade that would allow him to support himself and a family in the future. For the moment, he was just getting by working at the Grotto and that because he was the visionary's sister. Bernadette offered her brother excellent advice and she did so in a gentle, loving and firm tone.

My Dear Brother,

I heard that you worked at the Grotto a lot during vacation and that you might not return to Garaison this year. If you truly believe that God is not calling you to religious life, I strongly encourage you to decide on a trade. My dear friend, you must think of your future. I will be very disappointed if you keep working at the Grotto as you have been doing. You will not be able to find a job later on. But if you learn a trade and you like your work, you will always be able to make a living and get along.

My dear brother, please give this much thought with God in mind. I would not want you to become a priest just to make a position for yourself for anything in the world. No, I would rather you become a ragman.

Dear friend, I hope you understand that it is only my keen interest in your soul that makes me speak so. I will say it again: give this much thought and especially ask Our Lord and the Most Holy Virgin to show you their will.

I entreat you to be faithful to your religious obligations and obedient to Joseph and Marie. Send me news as soon as possible.

Adieu, dear godson. I close with an affectionate kiss.

Your devoted sister and godmother,

Sister Marie-Bernard Soubirous

"My weapons are prayer and sacrifice, and I shall pray and sacrifice until my last breath."

(To Pope Pius IX, December 17, 1876, final draft)

The following letter is the final version of four drafts of a letter addressed to Pope Pius IX. On December 16, the Bishop, Monsignor de Ladoue, who was leaving for Rome, visited Bernadette in the infirmary and asked her to write to the Holy Father to request his apostolic blessing. The humility expressed in this letter is emblematic of Bernadette and is in no way exceptional because it is addressed to the Holy Father. In addition, this letter evidences her vocation of "prayer and sacrifice".

From 1865 to 1871 there was a sort of children's crusade known by a variety of names such as "Zouaves of silence" and "the Pope's crusade". Children all over France dedicated themselves to fight for the protection of Pope Pius IX. Their arms consisted of silence, prayer, sacrifice and Holy Communion. On November 15, 1868, Monsignor Chigi, Papal Nuncio, visited Saint-Gildard and was told by the superior "we are soldiers of duty, Zouaves of prayer."

J. M. J.

Most Holy Father,

Despite my great desire to write Your Holiness, I, a poor little Sister, would never have dared take up my pen if our worthy bishop, Monsignor de Ladoue, had not encouraged me. Most Holy Father, I throw myself to my knees at your feet to pray for your apostolic blessing. Surely it will give renewed strength to my poor, weak soul.

At first, I was afraid of committing an indiscretion by writing to you. Then it occurred to me that Our Lord loves to hear the prayers of the little as much as the great, the poor as much as the rich and that he gives himself to each of us without distinction. This thought gave me courage and I am no longer afraid. Most Holy Father, I come to you as a poor little child freely and confidently approaches the most tender of Fathers. What can I do to show you my daughterly love, Most Holy Father? I can only continue to do what I have done all along: suffer and pray. Only a few years ago, I offered myself up as a little Zouave for Your Holiness. My weapons are prayer and sacrifice, and I shall pray and sacrifice until my last breath. In Heaven, sacrifice will no longer be possible, but my prayers will be even more powerful than they are in this land of exile.

Each day I pray to the Sacred Heart of Jesus and the Immaculate Heart of Mary to keep you with us for a long time since you make them so well known and loved. I have the sweet confidence that their Sacred Hearts will deign to grant this prayer, the dearest to my heart.

When I pray for the intentions of Your Holiness, it seems to me that surely the Holy Virgin must cast her maternal eye on you from Heaven, Most Holy Father, because you have proclaimed her Immaculate. I like to believe this good Mother loves you in a special way since four years after that proclamation she came to earth to say:

"I am the Immaculate Conception."

At the time, I did not know what this meant. I had never heard those words before. Since that time, when meditating on this, I have often said to myself: how good the Most Holy Virgin is. It seems that she came to confirm our Holy Father's words. This is what makes me believe that she must protect you in a very special way. I hope this good Mother will have pity on her children and that she will deign to crush the head of the cursed serpent beneath her feet once more and thus put an end to the cruel trials of the Holy Church and the sorrow of her August and Beloved Pontiff.

I very humbly kiss your feet and with the deepest respect I am,

> Most Holy Father,
> The very humble and very submissive daughter of Your Holiness.
>
> Sister Marie-Bernard Soubirous,
> Sister of Charity
> and of Christian Instruction of Nevers.

Nevers, December 17, 1876

"I struggled between fear and confidence; how could I, a poor, ignorant, little Sister who is so ill, dare to write the Most Holy Father?"

(December 17, 1876)

The following is the first draft of Bernadette's letter to Pope Pius IX.

Most Holy Father,

Had it not been for the encouragement of our worthy Bishop de Ladoue, I would never have dared to take up my pen to write Your Holiness. He said that the most certain means of receiving a blessing from the Holy Father was to write you and that he would be kind enough to send my letter. I struggled between fear and confidence; how could I, a poor, ignorant, little Sister who is so ill, dare to write the Most Holy Father? Never. But why such fear? He is my Father since he represents God on earth, God three times holy whom I dare to receive so often in my poor heart. It is because I am weak that I dare to receive God, who is strong. The same thinking encouraged me, Most Holy Father, to come and throw myself to my knees at your feet to ask for your apostolic blessing. It will surely be a source of renewed strength for my poor soul.

Most Holy Father, how can I express my great appreciation to you? I have long been Your Holiness' Zouave, however unworthy I may be. My weapons are prayer and sacrifice, and I shall pray and sacrifice until my last breath. In Heaven, sacrifice will no longer be possible, but my prayers will be even more powerful than they are in this land of exile. Every day I pray that the Sacred Heart of Jesus and the Immaculate Heart of Mary will keep you with us for many years to come since you have made them known and loved. Every time I pray for your intentions, it seems to me that the Most Holy Virgin surely looks down on you from Heaven, Most Holy Father, since you proclaimed her Immaculate. Four years later, this good Mother came to earth to say: I am the Immaculate. I did not know what that meant; I had never heard that word. When thinking about it since then, I say to myself that the Holy Virgin is so good; it seems she came to confirm the words of our Holy Father.

An Apostolic Blessing from Pope Pius IX

(Pope Pius IX to Bernadette's Bishop, Monsignor de Ladoue, January 3, 1877)

Pope Pius IX did indeed send his apostolic blessing to Bernadette and her entire Congregation. In addition, he sent her a small silver statue of Christ, which still exists and is kept at the Saint Bernadette Museum in Nevers.

Most Blessed Father,

Sister Marie-Bernard Soubirous, Sister of Charity and Christian Instruction of Nevers, humbly kneeling at the feet of Your Holiness, asks the Apostolic Blessing for herself and the Religious Community to which she belongs.

January 3, 1877

May God bless you and keep you in his care.

Pius PP. IX.

"I am praying to the Holy Child Jesus to give his holy love to her as a New Year's gift."

(To her Aunt Bernarde, December 27, 1876)

The cousins to whom Bernadette referred in this letter were her Aunt Bernarde's children: Pierre, Jules, Bernadette Nicolau (Bernadette's goddaughter), Lucie-Dominiquette and Marie-Anne. When she asked her cousins to remember her especially at the Grotto, she used the feminine form cousines, *referring to her Aunt Bernarde's daughters. Lucile was Lucile Pène, the daughter of her Aunt Basile.*

My Good and Dearest Godmother,

I do not want to let the New Year pass without wishing you a Happy New Year and assuring you that I pray often for your intentions and for the needs of your dear family. Good and dear Godmother, I have the sweet confidence that my cousins are and shall be an ever greater consolation to you by being meek and obedient to your good and charitable advice.

Ask my cousins [13] to remember me in their prayers, especially when they go to the Grotto. I have not heard from Lucile so I think she is a little angry with me. When I began to wonder why she had only written once from Saint-Pé, I realized that I had completely forgotten to answer her. I hope she does not hold it against me. It was not from indifference. It was just an oversight and I regret it enormously.

---

[13] The French words is *cousines*, indicating female cousins.

What is my dear little goddaughter up to? Does she love God? Is she good? I would like to have some New Year's gifts to send her, but I am so poor that I have nothing, absolutely nothing. Therefore I am praying to the Holy Child Jesus to give his love to her as her New Year's gift and also that he will make her and her sisters more and more pious. Please give her a big kiss for me.

My dear Godmother, you would be disappointed if I neglected to mention my health. I am better, but I am still having problems with my stomach. That is why it is taking so long to get back on my feet this time. They do everything possible for me here. I am embarrassed about how kind my Superiors and my companions are to me.

I close, my good and dearest Godmother, with an affectionate kiss for you and my dear cousins.

Your obedient goddaughter,

Sister Marie-Bernard Soubirous

——

"I beseech you, dearest sister, make the sacrifices God has asked of you through your dear children very generously. Let us always love and obey God's holy will."

(To her sister, Marie, December 27, 1876)

Constantly ill at this point, Bernadette was often completely bed-ridden. She loved her family and she longed to hear from them. Their silence made the physical distance between them even more difficult for her than it would have otherwise been and it made her worry about their reasons for being so reluctant to write. In spite of the fact that she said her health was better, "better" must be understood in context. Bernadette was so seriously ill that it was difficult for her even to write a letter. Surely she would have been consoled by a word from the brothers and sister she loved so dearly and about whom she worried. Bernadette feared that Marie was overcome with grief by the loss of her last little girl and in this letter she attempted to console her sister with her loving heart and wise spiritual advice.

The Sisters at Saint-Gildard needed permission to write letters, and the New Year was a season when they were easily granted this permission.

My Good and Dear Marie,

I have been looking forward to the first of the year to offer you and Joseph my best wishes for a Happy New Year, but at the same time to make this small reproach: it has been two months since I last wrote and I am very surprised that I still have not heard from you. I do not know what to make of your long silence, but I am very worried that you might be ill. I want you to be completely frank and tell me the reason without hiding anything.

I am extremely worried about Pierre. He has not written in such a long time. He must be very busy since he has not answered my last letter in which I asked him to tell me how you are. Nevertheless, it seems to me that he could have found a moment to write, even just a couple of lines. You can imagine how worried I am about him. I often wonder if he is at the house, what kind of work he is doing.

Please tell me if he is behaving and how he is spending his time.

Please let me hear from you as soon as possible. I am extremely worried about your health. I beseech you, dearest sister, make the sacrifices God has asked of you through your dear children very generously. Let us always love and obey God's holy will.

Please send news about Jean-Marie, if you have any that is. I am not writing Pierre since he does not answer my letters. My health is better, but I still cannot leave the infirmary except to attend holy Mass on Sunday.

Adieu, my good sister. I close with an affectionate kiss for all of you. Please pray for me.

Your devoted sister in the Sacred Hearts of Jesus and Mary,

Sister Marie-Bernard Soubirous

"Recently, when I remarked to the doctor about how long this has been going on, he turned on his heel and told me that I have a terrifying enemy."

(To Father Pomian, December 28, 1876)

Dear Father Pomian,

I do not want to let the first of the year go by without wishing you a Happy New Year. I hope so much to see you again in Nevers some time this year, if it be God's will. I will try to be a little nicer than I was last time. Every time I think about how impolite I was when you were here, I am so embarrassed. I apologize profusely. I hope you will not hold it against me.

What can I tell you about myself? Not much that is good. I am having problems with my stomach. For the last month, however, I have been able to keep a little more food down. Recently, when I remarked to the doctor about how long this has been going on, he turned on his heel and told me that I have a terrifying enemy. I am beginning to think that he has no idea what to make of me.

Please offer Mademoiselle Pomian my best wishes for a Happy New Year and ask her to pray for me.

Father, in closing, permit me to ask you to remember me in your holy prayers. I remember you in mine, even though they are so weak.

Our venerable Mother General and our dear Sisters ask me to offer you their best wishes and their respects.

Please accept my most sincere best wishes and the profound respects of a daughter.

Your grateful and obedient daughter in Our Lord,

Sister Marie-Bernard Soubirous

"I have been in my white chapel for more than a year."

(To Monsignor Peyramale, December 28, 1876)

The phrase, "I have been in my white chapel for more than a year", was a graceful, uncomplaining and matter-of-fact way of stating a fact: Bernadette had been bedridden for more than a year. While this was not the focus of the letter for Bernadette, it tells us much about her. Her focus was on Monsignor Peyramale's generosity to the orphans in Lourdes, her gratitude for his paternal care for her and her family over the years and her encouragement to him in his priesthood. For us, however, the contrast demonstrates her courage and generous heart.

The orphanage was the Mary Immaculate Orphanage, later renamed the Foyer des Bernadettes. The Bourbon Princess Mary-Immaculate had given an offering for an orphanage to Monsignor Langénieux, and since Bernadette had often expressed a desire for an orphanage in Lourdes, Monsignor chose to gratify that wish.

Monsignor,

How happy I am to see the season of the New Year approach when I am permitted to express my most sincere wishes for you, Monsignor. I am asking the Holy Child Jesus to keep you with your dear parishioners for many years to come so that your good example and your tireless and charitable zeal may edify them for a long time to come.

Monsignor, it was such a joy to hear that the work on your new Church has been advancing. I have not forgotten the little prayer for your intention every day that I promised you. Allow me to ask for an *Ave Maria* in return when you go to my dear Grotto. I certainly need it. I have been in my white chapel for more than a year. I gather the little strength I have to go to Mass on Sunday, with the help of an arm. I will be even happier this winter to be able to continue doing so, since last year it was impossible for me until May.

I hear that our dear little orphanage still has a big place in your heart and that you are often the purveyor, even going so far as to buy the wood for them. I did not need to hear that to know your generosity, Monsignor. I have received your paternal care too often myself to think you would do any less for these dear little orphans. Monsignor, I was already certain that they would find the heart of a true father in you.

Monsignor, permit me to express my great appreciation once more for all your kindness toward my family and me.

My dear Sister Nathalie sends her wishes for the New Year and her profound respect.

With great appreciation and respect,

> Your very humble and very obedient daughter in Our Lord,
>
> Sister Marie-Bernard Soubirous

"I was extremely surprised to read in your letter that you had been married."

(To Jean-Marie, the end of February, 1877)

Bernadette expressed the disappointment and sadness she felt when she discovered, only after the fact, that Jean-Marie was married. Only a fragment of this letter still exists in which she responded to his "rather cold" announcement of his marriage to Marie-Magdelaine Escalé on February 8, 1877.

... I assure you, I was extremely surprised to read in your letter that you had been married. I was even a little hurt. It is not that I was angry with you for marrying, not at all;

but it seems to me that it is only right that I should have been told two or three days beforehand. It would have been a source of happiness for me to unite my prayers with yours on that day to ask Our Lord and the Most Holy Virgin ...

Just between us, I found your letter rather cold. You told me your wife's name, but it seems to me that it would not be asking too much to tell me if she is from Lourdes and, more importantly, if she is from a Christian family. Dear friend, I hope you will be a little nicer the next time you write.

I am quite annoyed that Pierre has not continued his studies. He could have found a position in an office before long. He should try to. ...

"Father, please tell me if Pierre was really the one in the wrong."

(To Father Sempé, July 17, 1877)

Bernadette was extremely distressed when Mother Alexandrine Roques informed her that there were stories circulating in Lourdes about troubles in the Soubirous family. Although bedridden and far from the family home, Bernadette attempted to ascertain the truth. One of the stories was that as Marie and Joseph were returning from Poueyferré, they ran into Pierre who "ran away from them and then thumbed his nose". In actuality, the incident never took place.

On July 1, 1877, Pierre wrote an affectionate, yet matter-of-fact, letter to Bernadette in which he told her that Father Sempé

*had asked him about family troubles that were making Pierre's life
at home difficult. Pierre did not offer additional information to the
priest, but he did confirm what Father Sempé had heard. Father
invited Pierre to live with him and the other priests at the Grotto,
and he offered the seventeen-year-old a choice between learning the
trade of gardening or working in the chapel. Pierre preferred gardening.*

J. M. J.

†

Nevers, July 17, 1877

Very Reverend Father,

Allow me to extend my sincere gratitude for the paternal care and the great interest you have deigned to show
for my brother. I have been very worried about him for
some time. I tremble every time I consider the responsibility that I have for his soul and the fact that I will have to
account for my actions to Our Lord.

My dear Mother Alexandrine told me recently in her
letter that when Marie and Joseph were returning from Poueyferré, they ran into Pierre. Supposedly he took off running
and "thumbed his nose" at them. I do not understand why
he would have treated them so badly. Joseph said that he
had not said anything to him to provoke it. He said that,
on the contrary, he has always been very good to him.

I beg of you, Father, please, I beg of you, tell me if it was
really Pierre who was in the wrong. My dear Mother also said
in her letter that Joseph has seen Pierre with some rough looking young men, even since he has been staying with you.

Father, you understand that I have good reason to be concerned. I truly fear that he will end up going astray.

Please forgive me Father for enclosing two letters for my brothers with yours. Would you be kind enough to give them to my brothers yourself and to have them read them in your presence so that you can speak to them about this?

Very Reverend Father, please accept the most respectful and grateful feelings from

Your very humble servant,

Sister Marie-Bernard Soubirous

(To her brother, Jean-Marie, July 17, 1877)

My Dear Brother,

Apparently, you and your wife are the reason Pierre left home.

... Just imagine how it looks when strangers have to take care of our brother. Poor Jean-Marie, be careful, think ...

I am ashamed for all of you. What must the townspeople think to see you divided as you are, you who should provide a good example? ...

... now all of you are all worked up. I assure you, this is a source of great suffering for me to see the dissension among you when you could all live happily and contented, working hard and each one doing his part.

I am going to write Joseph, but I want to know what happened. Please give me the details ...

... P.S.—Please give my best to my godmother, her family, all our other uncles and aunts and their families.

(To her brother, Pierre, July 17, 1877)

Whenever Pierre wrote his beloved godmother, Bernadette, he always used vous, *the respectful form of* you. *This was appropriate inasmuch as she was fifteen years his senior, his godmother and the eldest sibling. Bernadette, however, used the more intimate* tu, *which was also appropriate. In this letter, however, Bernadette vacillated between the two. When she firmly reminded her brother of his responsibilities and expressed her displeasure with his behavior, she wrote* vous. *On the other hand, when she encouraged him in his new trade as gardener and expressed her affection for him, she returned naturally to the intimate* tu.

My Dear Pierre,

I am delighted to know that you are with the very Reverend Father Sempé, who will be able to give you excellent advice. I think you need it. I was told that you behaved most inappropriately to Marie and Joseph. What I have been told has hurt me deeply. I would never have supposed you capable of forgetting yourself to such a degree. What I heard was this: recently, you ran into Joseph and Marie on the road to Poueyferré and you . . .

. . . ran off and then thumbed your nose at them. If this is true, please go to them and ask their forgiveness for your lack of respect and the pain you caused them.

Is this how you respond to the excellent upbringing you received with the good Fathers? Do you think you express your gratitude and reward them by profiting so badly from their good example and the education they offered you so generously?

Do you think God and the Most Holy Virgin are happy and glorified by that? No, of course not. If you love them, you will prove it by behaving in an irreproachable manner hereafter. You are the youngest in the family, so you owe respect to Marie, Joseph and Jean-Marie. I want you all to love each other ... Father Sempé ... his good counsel will do you good, I am sure.

I am very pleased that you are learning to be a gardener; a trade like that will serve you well, especially if you like it. I implore you not to spend time with young people who have a bad influence on you. It will do you harm without you even suspecting it. Love your work and you will see how much good it will do you.

Dear Pierre, I hope this will be the first and the last time I have to reproach you this way ...

P.S. My health is better. I take a walk in the garden every day to regain my strength.

Adieu.

In a letter dated July 24, 1877, Father Sempé reassured Bernadette that there was no truth to the story of Pierre "thumbing his nose at Marie and Joseph". Father Sempé reassured Bernadette that this "dear child is good and pious" and that he cried when he read Bernadette's letter. Joseph was the one who was at fault for whatever difficulties there were in the family. Jean-Marie's stubbornness did not help the situation, but she needed not worry about his behavior. "The divisions are not serious and neither God nor the public has reason to be offended."

In an affectionate and respectful letter also dated July 24, 1877, Pierre explained the situation to his sister. He had not wanted to tell her about the strife between himself and Joseph for fear of hurting her. There never was an incident on the road from Poueyferré, and Pierre explained that he had never been disrespectful to Marie or Joseph. About three months earlier, Pierre was suffering from "nervous rheumatism" and was unable to stand up straight. Whenever Pierre and Joseph met, Joseph would make fun of Pierre's affliction by saying: "Adieu, Monsieur Duroi." (There was a hunchbacked man by the name of Monsieur Duroi who worked at the Grotto.) Pierre finally lost patience with the "joke" and said to Joseph: "You know my baptismal name. Would you please call me by my name?" By the time Bernadette heard the rumor of Pierre "thumbing his nose" at his sister and brother-in-law, the unpleasantness was over and everyone was getting along.

"We must love God's will, since nothing happens that he does not permit; otherwise, I think I would hold it against my dear Lourdais a little bit for hurting him."

(To Father Pomian, September 15, 1877)

On September 8, 1877, the feast of the Nativity of the Holy Virgin, Monsignor Peyramale, Bernadette's long-time confidant and beloved priest, died suddenly. Bernadette was "crushed" by the news, but she was consoled in knowing that "the Most Holy Virgin came for our good Father the day of her Nativity to reward him for the sacrifices and the difficult trials he accepted and suffered for love of her." She was also consoled by the knowledge that her beloved Father Pomian was with him and that he was able to receive last rites in full consciousness.

Dear Father Pomian,

I am so sorry I was not able to write you sooner, but I was crushed by the sudden death of our dear and venerable Monsignor Peyramale. What a cruel loss for the people of Lourdes! If they do not understand that his zeal for the glory of God and the salvation of their own souls hastened the death of our dear and good pastor, they are most ungrateful. I have heard that the sadness he felt about his new church contributed a great deal to his death. It would not surprise me; the work he had begun so well meant so much to him. We must love God's will, since nothing happens that he does not permit; otherwise, I think I would hold it against my dear Lourdais a little bit for hurting him. He was such a good Father who took such a keen and fatherly interest in them. I heard the devastating news on the day of the Nativity of the Most Holy Virgin. At nine o'clock, my dear Sister Nathalie came looking for me in the choir and told me we had just received a telegram announcing that Monsignor Peyramale was very close to death. The next day, a second telegram announced his death. Father, it is impossible to express the grief I felt at that moment! But as great as my grief was, just as great was the sweet consolation I felt when I read that our beloved Monsignor had the joy of receiving last rites in full consciousness and that during his last moments you were there to help him, Father, the friend of his heart, his faithful and zealous servant.

The Most Holy Virgin came for our good Father the day of her Nativity to reward him for the sacrifices and the difficult trials he accepted and suffered for love of her.

Father, I know that the sudden and unexpected death of our worthy and venerable Pastor must be a cruel blow to you. The respect and attachment you felt for him tells me how enormous the emptiness his passing must be for you. The only thing that can ease our pain is the thought that we have one more advocate in Heaven.

For the last three months, my health has grown much stronger and I am able to participate in many of the exercises of the Community. I take walks and I have a very good appetite.

Father, please give me a small place in your prayers and holy sacrifices. I have the honor of being your very humble and obedient child.

Respectfully,

Sister Marie-Bernard Soubirous

P.S. Father, please extend my condolences to your sister.

"I am happy to learn that the Lord Bishop deigned to consider making my little brother his valet."

(To Father Sempé, January 15, 1878)

Father Sempé's kindness and generosity to Bernadette's loved ones was evident and this was shown yet again. Through his influence,

Pierre was chosen to be the valet de chambre *to the Bishop of Tarbes. In his brief letter announcing this news, Father Sempé's tone was simple and matter-of-fact, but he also expressed great sensitivity to what he knew to be Bernadette's concern for her family, especially her beloved brother and godson, Pierre. His observation that "Pierre is still very naïve and very good" was a balm to his loving sister. His closing words are more than just a formulaic expression of* politesse. *They reveal Father Sempé's own humility before this humble nun: "We are praying for you at the Grotto; please pray a little for your devoted servant." He was indeed devoted to Bernadette and he served her and her loved ones time and time again.*

My Very Reverend Father,

I am so sorry that I was not able to express my gratitude to you sooner for your kindness in taking such an interest in my young brother. I hope he will always accept your good and charitable advice obediently.

I am happy to learn that the Lord Bishop deigned to consider making my little brother his valet. I hope this dear child will respond to the trust the Lord Bishop has condescended to show him by conducting himself well.

Very Reverend Father, permit me to thank you for your holy prayers at my dear Grotto. I surely need them, for I have been sick for the last two months. I am not allowed to attend Holy Mass on Sunday. The sacrifice is great, but I must resign myself to it.

Very Reverend Father, with respect and enormous gratitude, I remain your very humble servant,

Sister Marie-Bernard Soubirous

"If God asks of us the sacrifice of not seeing each other again on earth, let us make it joyfully."

(To her brother, Pierre, October 7, 1878)

With her death a mere six months away, Bernadette was permitted to make her perpetual vows, which she affectionately referred to as "my great religious vows".

Pierre was heartbroken to learn that Bernadette was dying and that they would never again see each other "on earth"; however, she encouraged him to make the sacrifice "joyfully". She was correct in saying that her letters "are circulating everywhere." Pilgrims were avid for anything belonging to her, including scraps of old school lessons, and evidently there was no dearth of people willing to provide them.

Bernadette became expert in embroidery and in making lace; there is still in existence many a "Sacred Heart" similar to the one she sent her brother with this letter. The museum at Saint-Gildard owns two exquisite albs fashioned by Bernadette.

My Dear Brother,

When our venerable Mother General gave me your dear letter, she almost scolded me for having left you without news of my health for so long. I am happy to be able to report that my strength is returning little by little. I am still limping a little, but I quit using the crutches three months ago. Don't worry. It is not serious, just a little sciatic pain in the knee. It did hurt, it is true, but it is over now.

Dear friend, I do not want to let my letter go without sharing my happiness with you: I received the signal favor of being allowed to make my great religious vows on the 15th of September,[14] the day consecrated to the Seven Sorrows of the Most Holy Virgin. I am so unworthy of such a great grace. Help me with your prayers to thank Our Lord and the Most Holy Virgin a little.

This is why I write you so rarely: I have been told that my letters are circulating everywhere. It hurt me so much to discover this and if it happens again I will not write anyone anymore.

As for your tears, I assure you that when I read your letter I felt the same way. I had to use my handkerchief. I understand what your good heart is feeling. Come on, dear friend, let us both be generous. If God asks of us the sacrifice of not seeing each other again on earth, let us make it joyfully.

Please give my deepest respects to his Lord Bishop and ask him to accept my gratitude for the great interest he deigns to take in you.

Adieu, dear brother, I close with an affectionate kiss.

Your devoted sister who will meet you in the Sacred Hearts of Jesus and Mary,

Sister Marie-Bernard Soubirous

P.S. I am sending you a little Sacred Heart that I made. Keep it with you.

[14] The date was actually September 22.

"If you want God to grant you the grace you want so much to come see me, be very good, very generous."

(To Pierre, January 5, 1879)

Through the generosity of a pilgrim, Jean-Marie had managed to travel to Nevers, where he and Bernadette enjoyed a long conversation. The following letter to Pierre suggests that although she had been insistent that Jean-Marie let her know when he arrived safely back in Lourdes, he neglected to do so. Poor Pierre, who loved his sister and godmother tenderly and devotedly, had not seen her since she left Lourdes when he was only seven years old. He desperately wanted to see her one last time, but this proved to be impossible. As she did in so many of her letters to her family, Bernadette expressed her concern for their spiritual and physical well-being, and as always, she offered motherly advice to her little brother and godson.

My Dearest Brother,

I received your letter with such great pleasure, as you can easily imagine since you know how tender my affection for you has always been. I was also happy to know that Jean-Marie had arrived home safely, for I was anxious to have news of him. I was so insistent that he write me as soon as he arrived that I was afraid something had happened to him.

Our venerable Mother informed me that Marie is sick. I am very distressed about it, especially since it has already been a while, and I still do not know if it is serious or not. I am anxious to know how she is. She might have been annoyed that Jean-Marie came to see me without telling her. If you could find out, without letting her know that I spoke to you about it, I would appreciate it. If you want God to grant you the grace you want so much (according to what you told me) to come see me, be very good, very generous. I feel better. I am coughing less now that the weather has improved a little. Our venerable Mother wanted me to make a novena to Our Lady of Lourdes to ask for my healing. It will end on Saturday. Please join me in this intention and ask the rest of the family to do so also. If I am healed, please go to the Grotto in thanksgiving for such a great favor.

Please offer my profound respects to the Lord Bishop and wish him a Happy New Year for me. . . . If you will also be my interpreter with the family, tell them that they can always count on my most ardent good wishes for them.

I leave you with these fond feelings, beloved brother, until I have the pleasure of seeing you. A thousand wishes for happiness, adieu pour Dieu.

Your sister who loves you,

Sister Marie-Bernard

"Everything that affects you interests me, for I have such tender affection for all of you."

(To Bernadette Nicolau, January 11, 1879)

This letter to fifteen-year-old Bernadette Nicolau was Bernadette's last existing letter. She was seriously disappointed that her young goddaughter had to leave school and go to work. Her father's death four years earlier was the reason: the family needed the income. Bernadette, who was too ill to write at this point, dictated this letter to another Sister who wrote it for her.

My Dear Little Goddaughter,

Your letter gave me such pleasure. Everything that affects you interests me, for I have such tender affection for all of you. Thank you for your prayers. As for me, I pray that you will continue to be good, obedient and pious. I am sorry to see you leave school while you are still so young. Now is the time when you could profit from it the most since you are more at the age of reason.

Well, no one is obliged to do the impossible; if you need to help Godmother, you must make the sacrifice. Tell your Mama that I think of her in my suffering. I often offer it to God for her needs, as well as your needs and those of your brothers. Godmother intended to send me something with my brother, and I thank her for it. I am as grateful for it as if I had received it.

When you see my dear Mother and the Sisters, please wish them Happy New Year for me and assure them that I still have such wonderful memories of them.

Adieu, my dear child. I am sending a very tender kiss from your godmother who loves you.

Sister Marie-Bernard Soubirous

P.S. You will laugh at my absentmindedness, but I am too tired to begin again, adieu.

CHAPTER 7

"Pray for me, a poor sinner"
April 16, 1879

The following is Sister Nathalie Portat's account of the death of Saint Bernadette.

At 7:00 P.M., Sister X was in the chapel before the altar of the Holy Virgin, asking our divine Mother to protect her beloved child, whose condition was becoming more and more critical.

At the end of her prayer, the Religious felt compelled to go see the patient, who upon seeing her, said: "My dear Sister, I am afraid ... I have received so many graces and I have profited from them so little! ..." "All the merits of the Heart of Jesus are ours, Sister X said to her; offer them to God to pay your debts and in thanksgiving for all his blessings." Then, after having promised the patient to help her always to thank the Most Holy Virgin for the favors with which she had condescended to honor her, the Religious added some words in a low voice.... "Ah! Thank you", said the patient, who seemed relieved, as if a great weight had been lifted from her.

The next day, April 16 at around 3:00 P.M. the patient seemed to be tortured by an inexpressible interior agony.

The Sisters who worked in the infirmary were alarmed and rushed to sprinkle holy water on the dying woman several times, suggesting holy invocations to her. The patient seized her crucifix, contemplated it lovingly for a moment, then she slowly kissed the wounds of Christ, one by one.[1]

At the same moment, Sister X entered the infirmary and approached the dying woman, who seemed absorbed in contemplating her crucifix. All of a sudden, she lifted her head, stretched her arms toward Sister X and, looking at her with an indescribable expression, said: "My dear Sister, pardon me . . . Pray for me . . . Pray for me."

Sister X and the two nurses fell to their knees to pray. The patient joined their invocations, which she repeated in a low voice. Then, she collected herself for a moment, her head tilted toward the Sister who was at her left, and with an expression of sadness and supreme abandon, she lifted her eyes to Heaven, stretched out her arms in the form of a cross and cried out: "My God!" . . .

An involuntary shudder of respect mixed with fear seized the three Sisters, who were still kneeling. One of them supported the dying woman's arms, which were still stretched out . . . Finally, she dropped her arms and joined in the prayers of her companions again. At the words of the Angelic Salutation: "Holy Mary, Mother of God", the dying woman revived and, in a voice full of conviction, a voice that in her final moments expressed her profound humility and her daughterly confidence in the Immaculate Virgin, she twice repeated: "Holy Mary, Mother of God, pray for me, a poor sinner."

---

[1] This crucifix had been brought from Rome by Msgr. de Ladoue, Bishop of Nevers, in 1877 as a gift to Bernadette; it is currently at the motherhouse in Nevers.

Death was approaching . . . A terrifying struggle seemed to have begun again in that innocent and privileged soul. Surely God wanted to make her more closely resemble our divine Savior dying on the Cross . . .

The patient tossed restlessly for a moment and then silently renewed her plea to Sister X two more times, stretching out her arms to the Sister, her eyes fastened on her. Deeply moved, the Religious tried to understand what the dying woman wanted, asking with her expression: "Why are you stretching out your arms to me? What do you want of me?" The dying woman answered Sister X's thoughts in a strong voice: "I want you to help me. . . ."

Sister X then remembered the promise she had made the day before.

A few moments later, the patient motioned that she wanted something to drink; She made a large sign of the cross, took the bottle they gave her, drank a few drops and, inclining her head to one side, she gently rendered up her virginal soul to her Creator, while her companions were repeating this invocation: Jesus, Mary, Joseph, have pity on her, protect her.

Unbeknownst to them, they had fulfilled Sister Marie-Bernard's desire for the grace to die repeating the sweet names of Jesus, Mary, Joseph.

CHRONOLOGY OF THE APPARITIONS OF OUR LADY TO BERNADETTE SOUBIROUS
February 11, 1858–July 16, 1858

First apparition

Thursday, February 11
Bernadette saw a beautiful young Lady at the Grotto of Massabielle.

On Thursday, February 11, 1858, Bernadette Soubirous went to the Grotto of Massabielle with two other girls. When the two girls crossed the millstream and left Bernadette alone on the other shore, she suddenly heard "a noise like a sudden gust of wind". When she looked up at the Grotto, she saw a beautiful young Lady surrounded in light standing in a niche. Seized with fear, Bernadette took her Rosary out of her pocket and tried to make the Sign of the Cross, but she could not raise her hand to her forehead. When the Lady made the sign of the Cross with her Rosary, Bernadette's fear vanished. She knelt and prayed the Rosary in the presence of the beautiful Lady. When Bernadette finished praying the Rosary, the vision suddenly disappeared.

Second apparition

Sunday, February 14
Bernadette emptied an entire bottle of holy water on the Lady.

Sensing an inner call, Bernadette felt compelled to return to the Grotto the following Sunday. Armed with a small bottle of holy water, Bernadette and her friends arrived at the Grotto, and they all knelt and began to pray the Rosary. When the beautiful Lady appeared again, Bernadette quickly sprinkled her with holy water and said: "If you are from God stay, but if not, go away." The more Bernadette sprinkled her with holy water, the more she smiled and bowed her head. Bernadette was "overcome with fear, so she hurriedly splashed her until the bottle was empty". She began praying the Rosary again, and when she finished the Lady vanished.

Third apparition

Thursday, February 18
"Would you have the grace to come here for fifteen days?"

The young visionary went to the Grotto equipped with paper and pen. After praying a few Hail Marys, Bernadette saw the same vision as before. Offering the Lady the paper and pen, she said: "If you have something to say to me, would you be kind enough to write it down?" The Lady smiled and answered that it would not be necessary. Then, addressing Bernadette with more respect than anyone ever had shown her before, the beautiful Lady asked: *"Would you have the grace to return here for fifteen days?"* Bernadette accepted. She also told her: *"I do not promise to make you happy in this world, but in the other."*

Fourth apparition

Friday, February 19
The Lady was silent.

Bernadette took with her a lighted candle that had been blessed. Ever since that day, pilgrims have been lighting candles before the Grotto.

Fifth apparition

Saturday, February 20
The Lady taught Bernadette a personal prayer.

It is believed that this was the day when the Lady taught Bernadette a prayer that was "for her only." At the end of this vision, Bernadette was filled with sadness.

Sixth apparition

Sunday, February 21
Aquéro.

The Lady appeared early in the morning. Later that day, Police Commissioner Dominique Jacomet interrogated Bernadette. In response to his question: "Who is this Lady?" she said "*Aquéro*", patois for "that one".

Seventh apparition

Tuesday, February 23
The Lady told Bernadette three secrets.

According to tradition, this was the day when the Lady told Bernadette three secrets that she was not supposed to divulge to anyone.

Eighth apparition

Wednesday, February 24
"Penance! Penance! Penance!"

With the eighth apparition, the penitential phase of the visions began. On this day, the Lady said to Bernadette: *"Penance! Penance! Penance!"* She asked Bernadette to *"pray to God for sinners"*. In addition, she asked Bernadette: *"Would you kiss the ground for the conversion of sinners?"*

Ninth apparition

Thursday, February 25
"Go drink from the spring and wash there."

During the ninth apparition the Lady said to Bernadette: *"Go drink from the spring and wash there."* Bernadette started toward the Gave River, but the Lady indicated that she meant a place under the great rock wall that makes the Grotto. All Bernadette saw there was a little mud; three times she tried to drink it, and three times it came back up. On the fourth try she was able to keep some of it down. The Lady then asked her to *"eat some of the grass that is near the spring"*.

Again the Lady asked Bernadette to *"pray for sinners"*, and she repeated the words *"Penance! Penance! Penance!"*

Tenth apparition

Saturday, February 27
Penance.

Bernadette prayed, she repeated the acts of penance that she had performed during previous apparitions and she drank from the spring.

Eleventh apparition

Sunday, February 28
Penance.

In the presence of over one thousand onlookers, Bernadette crawled on her hands and knees as a sign of penance. She prayed and kissed the ground.

Twelfth apparition

Monday, March 1
The first miracle occurred at the Grotto of Massabielle.

There were approximately fifteen hundred people present during this early morning apparition. Later that night, a Lourdaise woman by the name of Catherine Latapie returned to the Grotto; when she bathed her paralyzed arm in the spring, she was cured of her paralysis.

Thirteenth apparition

Tuesday, March 2
"Go ask the priests to have the people come here in procession and tell them to have a chapel built."

It was during this thirteenth apparition that the Lady said to Bernadette: *"Go ask the priests to have the people come here in procession and tell them to have a chapel built."* When Bernadette told this to Father Peyramale, he told her to ask the Lady for a miracle: if she wanted a chapel built, she should make the wild rose bush at the Grotto bloom in the middle of winter. He also wanted to know the Lady's name.

Fourteenth apparition

Wednesday, March 3
The Lady renewed her request for a chapel.

When Bernadette arrived at the Grotto at around seven in the morning the Lady did not appear. After school, Bernadette felt drawn to the Grotto and this time the vision returned. Once again she asked the Lady her name, but as always her only response was a gentle smile. During this apparition, the Lady repeated her request for a chapel to be built.

Fifteenth apparition

Thursday, March 4
The crowd expected a miracle that did not occur.

Between six and eight thousand people were present during this early morning apparition, and everyone was expecting to witness a miracle. This was the last day of the original fifteen days that the Lady had requested during the third apparition, and this would be the fifteenth apparition. Nevertheless, it was not the fifteenth time that the Lady would appear after having asked Bernadette to come to the Grotto for fifteen days. The Lady would indeed appear three more times, keeping her implied promise to appear fifteen more times after the third apparition. During this apparition the Lady was silent, and the anticipated miracle did not occur. The fifteenth apparition was a long one, lasting for about forty-five minutes. After this apparition, Bernadette did not feel the inner call to return to the Grotto again for another three weeks.

Sixteenth apparition

Thursday, March 25, Solemnity of the Annunciation of the Lord
"I am the Immaculate Conception."

After three weeks without an apparition, on Thursday, March 25, the Solemnity of the Annunciation of the Lord, Bernadette felt an irresistible desire to go to the Grotto. During this apparition, Bernadette asked the Lady her name three times in a row; yet again, she only responded with a smile. It was only when Bernadette dared to ask a fourth time that the vision disclosed her identity. Looking up to Heaven, her hands folded as in prayer, she answered: *"I am the Immaculate Conception."*[1] These were the last words the Holy Virgin spoke to Bernadette.

---

[1] The Holy Virgin said in patois: "*Que soy Immaculada Conceptiou.*"

Seventeenth apparition

Wednesday, April 7
Dr. Douzous witnessed the miracle of the candle.

Around six o'clock in the morning, Bernadette felt the mysterious call to the Grotto. While in ecstasy there, she cupped her hand so closely around her candle to keep the wind from extinguishing the flame that everyone was certain she would have a very serious burn as a result. Dr. Pierre-Romain Douzous, a Lourdes physician, was present, and upon examining Bernadette after the apparition, he found no sign of a burn.

Eighteenth apparition

Friday, July 16, Feast of Our Lady of Mount Carmel
"I had never seen her so beautiful."

On Friday, July 16th, Bernadette felt the inner call to go to the Grotto; however, it had been blocked off by the authorities. Undaunted, she proceeded to the prairie across from the Gave River and knelt to pray. As she gazed across the river to the Grotto, the Holy Virgin appeared to her one last time. "It seemed to me that I was at the Grotto, at the same distance as the other times. All I could see was the Virgin. I had never seen her so beautiful."

BERNADETTE'S FAMILY

Bernadette's Father
François Soubirous: July 7, 1807–March 4, 1871.

Bernadette's Mother
Louise (Castérot) Soubirous: September 28, 1825–December 8, 1866.

Bernadette and her Brothers and Sisters

1. Saint Bernadette (baptized Bernarde-Marie Soubirous, known in religion as Sister Marie-Bernard Soubirous):[1] January 7, 1844–April 16, 1879.
2. Jean Soubirous: February 13, 1845–April 10, 1845.
3. Marie Soubirous (also called Toinette): September 19, 1846–October 13, 1892.
4. Jean-Marie Soubirous: December 10, 1848–January 4, 1851.
5. Jean-Marie Soubirous (called Brother Marie-Bernard from 1870 to approximately 1873): May 13, 1851–February 27, 1919.
6. Justin Soubirous: February 28, 1855–February 1, 1865.
7. Bernard-Pierre Soubirous (called Pierre, Saint Bernadette's godson): September 10, 1859–February 2, 1931.
8. Jean Soubirous: February 4, 1864–September 11, 1864.

---

[1] Bernard is the masculine form and Bernarde is the feminine form. Bernadette was baptized Bernarde-Marie, the feminine form. Her name in religion was Sister Marie-Bernard, the masculine form in honor of St. Bernard.

9.   A little girl was born in January 1866 and died a few minutes after her birth. Her birth was not registered.

Paternal Branch: Bernadette's Aunts and Uncles

1.   Thècle Soubirous: April 30, 1803–February 11, 1882.
2.   Jeanne-Marie Soubirous (called Jeanne): April 24, 1804–March 3, 1858.
3.   Jean-Marie Soubirous: September 5, 1805–May 18, 1845.
4.   François Soubirous (Saint Bernadette's father): July 7, 1807–March 4, 1871.
5.   Rémi Soubirous: December 17, 1808–July 15, 1809.
6.   Julie Soubirous: June 7, 1810–December 2, 1811.
7.   Pierre Soubirous: May 2, 1812–December 18, 1840.
8.   Jean Soubirous: born approximately 1813–May 19, 1858.
9.   Jeanne-Marie Soubirous[2] (called Marie): December 23, 1814—no date of death available.

Maternal Branch: Bernadette's Aunts and Uncles

1.   Bernarde Castérot (Saint Bernadette's godmother): October 10, 1823–January 31, 1907.
2.   Louise Castérot (Saint Bernadette's mother): September 28, 1825–December 8, 1866.
3.   Basile Castérot: May 21, 1828–June 22, 1913.
4.   Jean-Marie Castérot: October 23, 1830–July 13, 1878.
5.   Julien Castérot: February 16, 1833–September 7, 1835.
6.   Bernarde-Françoise Castérot: December 2, 1835–February 4, 1838.
7.   Lucile Castérot: May 5, 1839–March 16, 1871.

---

[2] It was not uncommon in the region to give two living children the same baptismal name.

IMPORTANT DATES IN THE LIFE
OF BERNADETTE

1844

January 7	Bernadette Soubirous was born at the Boly Mill in Lourdes, France. She was the first daughter of François Soubirous, a miller, and his wife Louise Soubirous (née Castérot).
January 9	Bernadette was baptized.

1858

ca. January 27	Bernadette felt so compelled to learn her Catechism and make her First Holy Communion that she left Bartès, where she had been tending sheep at the home of her former nanny, and she walked home to Lourdes.
February 11, 1858 to July 16, 1858	Bernadette experienced eighteen visions of the Holy Virgin Mary at the Grotto of Massabielle.

1860

July	Bernadette began living with the Sisters of Charity and Christian Instruction (the Sisters of Nevers) at the Hospice in Lourdes, where she was learning to read and write.

1862

April 28   Bernadette received Last Rites[1] for
                            the first time when she was on the
                            verge of dying from pneumonia. She
                            began recovering very quickly after
                            receiving the sacrament.

1866

End of 1865 to   Bernadette was received as a
Beginning of 1866   postulant with the Community at the
                            Hospice. She worked as a nurse's aid
                            in the infirmary and she also helped
                            with the children.

July 4   Accompanied by Mother Alexandrine
                            Roques, Mother Ursule Court and
                            two other postulants, Léontine Mouret
                            and Marie Larrotis, Bernadette left
                            Lourdes to live with the Sisters of
                            Charity and Christian Instruction in
                            Nevers.

July 7   At around ten thirty at night, Berna-
                            dette arrived in Nevers.

July 29   Bernadette received the religious habit
                            of the Congregation of the Sisters of
                            Charity and Christian Instruction of
                            Nevers. She was given the name Sis-
                            ter Marie-Bernard.

---

[1] In the nineteenth century, the Sacrament of Anointing was called Extreme
Unction or Last Rites; it was administered only when death appeared
immanent.

ca. August 14	Bernadette began working in the infirmary as a nurse's aid.
Early September	Bernadette fell ill and remained bedridden until February 1867.
October 25	Bernadette was given Last Rites for the second time. In addition, she professed her vows *in articulo mortis*, after which she improved. She told Mother Vauzou, who was watching over her, "No, I shall not die tonight."
December 8	Louise Soubirous, Saint Bernadette's mother, died.

1867

October 30	Bernadette made her religious profession with the other novices.

1869

Easter	Bernadette was ill and confined to bed.
November 6	The Journal of the Congregation notes: "Sister Marie-Bernard is sick. She is chronically ill."

1870

February or March	Jean-Marie, Bernadette's brother, entered the novitiate with the Brothers of Christian Instruction of Ploërmel (the Brothers of Ploërmel).
April 12	Bernadette was sick and in the infirmary.

June 27	Jean-Marie received his habit and was given the name Brother Marie-Bernard.

1871

March 4	François Soubirous, Bernadette's father, died.
June 27	After his novitiate, Brother Marie-Bernard was sent to school in Eauze. Three years later, he left religious life permanently.

1873

January 17	Bernadette suffered from a very severe asthma attack and was transferred to the Sainte-Julienne Infirmary. Her illness lasted for three months.
Easter, April 13	Bernadette had recovered enough to go to Easter Mass; afterward, she suffered a relapse and had to remain in bed for another two weeks.
June 3	Bernadette received Last Rites for the third time.
October	Bernadette was relieved of her duties in the infirmary because of her illness.

1874

Early January	Since Bernadette was a little stronger, she began working as an assistant to the sacristan. This work was less strenuous than her work in the infirmary;

however, she continued to work in the infirmary when she was well enough.

1875

October	Bernadette's only work henceforth was what she called her "job of being sick". Except on rare occasions, she was not able to attend Mass again until 1876.
November 19	The Journal of the Congregation reads: "We are very worried about her condition."

1876

July	A slight improvement allowed Bernadette to attend Mass.
December 16–17	From her bed in the infirmary, Bernadette wrote to Pope Pius IX to ask for his apostolic blessing.

1877

September 8	Monsignor Peyramale died.
September	Bernadette was too ill to make her perpetual vows with the Sisters with whom she had made her first religious profession.
End of September	A slight improvement in her health allowed Bernadette to take part in the religious life of the Community.
December	Bernadette was completely bedridden yet again.

1878

July to October	Bernadette's health improved slightly.
September 22	Bernadette made her perpetual vows.
October	Ill again, Bernadette was back in the infirmary.

1879

March 28	Bernadette was given Last Rites for the fourth and last time.
April 16, 1879	Bernadette died.

1925

June 14, 1925	Bernadette was beatified.

1933

December 8, 1933	On the Solemnity of the Immaculate Conception, Saint Bernadette was canonized by Pope Pius XI at Saint Peter's in Rome.

ABBREVIATIONS

OJR   Pierre Olivaint, S.J. *Journal des retraites annuelles, 1860–1870.* 2nd ed. 2 vols. Albanel, 1873.

ESB   André Ravier, S.J., ed. *Les Écrits de Sainte Bernadette et sa voie spirituelle.* 3rd ed. Paris: P. Lethielleux, 1980.

GLA   Grotte de Lourdes (account of the apparitions from the Liasse Déal).

GLB   Grotte de Lourdes (accounts of the police interrogations and the visit to Father Peyramale from the Liasse Déal).

GLC   Carnet à la Reine·du Ciel (from the Liasse Déal). *Journal Dedicated to the Queen of Heaven* was not the only notebook that Bernadette began in which she intended to write an account of the apparitions. She began another one entitled *Carnet à la Reine du Ciel* (Notebook to the Queen of Heaven).